Praise for *The Church of Mercy* by Pope Francis

"This collection offers fascinating insight into the mind and heart of someone who has rapidly become one of the world's most beloved public figures."
—Publishers Weekly

"Refreshingly humane, focusing on people rather than institutions. Admirers of Francis and students of Church history alike will find this a useful introduction to the pontiff's thought."
—Kirkus Reviews

"A refreshing book, a true treasure chest of wisdom, which will both comfort and unsettle any attentive reader."
—Englewood Review of Books

"I can't even tell you the sense of wonder and gratitude I am feeling reading The Church of Mercy. *Every Christian in at least the western world should read this man . . . at least read enough to know what Christianity has come upon or been given or will be watching develop over the next few years. This man sees, and is of, the Kingdom of God."*
—Phyllis Tickle, author of *The Great Emergence*

Praise for *Walking with Jesus* by Pope Francis

*"Magnificent. A beautiful invitation by a truly holy man to meet
the one at the center of his life: Jesus Christ."*

—James Martin, SJ, author of *Jesus: A Pilgrimage*

*"Pope Francis knows that the encounter with Jesus Christ puts our
lives on a new path. Our life of faith is a journey that we are
making with Jesus—walking with him, sharing his life, traveling in
the company of brothers and sisters who have accepted his invitation:
'Follow me.' In this inspiring book, our Holy Father offers us bread
for the journey—to deepen our friendship with Jesus and our
fellowship in continuing his mission of mercy in our world."*

—Most Reverend José H. Gomez, Archbishop of Los Angeles

*"A wonderfully inspiring and stirring resource capturing the depth of
Pope Francis's magnificent vision and mission. His powerful message
speaks of the richness of Catholic story and tradition.* Walking with
Jesus: A Way Forward for the Church *is an exceptional source of
wisdom and guidance for all involved in the ministry of
religious education."*

—Edith Prendergast, RSC, Director of Religious Education,
Archdiocese of Los Angeles

*"What a wonderful addition to our knowledge of the fresh and
inspiring message of a revolutionary pope from 'the ends of
the earth!'"*

—Allan Figueroa Deck, SJ, Casassa Chair and Professor of
Theology, Loyola Marymount University

Praise for *The Joy of Discipleship* by Pope Francis

"The capacity for joy takes its root in hope. Pope Francis is our generation's prophet of hope and thus our prophet of joy. This is him at his best, befuddling our unhappy categories, offering a vision of hope and mercy, and showing us in his own person the joy found in an earthy, cheerful discipleship."
—Ronald Rolheiser OMI, President, Oblate School of Theology

"According to Pope Francis, God's compassionate love for us and our responsibility to love one another, especially the poor and marginalized, are central to evangelization. God's love fills us with joy, which we want to share with others. Francis preaches the Gospel, not the catechism. He is more concerned about how we live our faith than how we explain it."
—Thomas J. Reese, SJ, Senior Analyst, *National Catholic Reporter* and author of *Inside the Vatican: The Politics and Organization of the Catholic Church*

"If one is seeking inspiration from Pope Francis, The Joy of Discipleship *is the best compilation out there."*
—Mark E. Thibodeaux, SJ, author of *God's Voice Within* and *Reimagining the Ignatian Examen*

Other Loyola Press Books by Pope Francis

The Church of Mercy: A Vision for the Church

Walking with Jesus: A Way Forward for the Church

The Joy of Discipleship: Reflections from Pope Francis on Walking with Christ

Reflections from Pope Francis on Living Our Faith

Embracing
the Way of Jesus

by POPE FRANCIS

Edited and compiled by
James P. Campbell

Foreword by ARCHBISHOP JOSEPH E. KURTZ

LOYOLAPRESS.
A JESUIT MINISTRY
Chicago

LOYOLA PRESS.
A JESUIT MINISTRY

3441 N. Ashland Avenue
Chicago, Illinois 60657
(800) 621-1008
www.loyolapress.com

Cover art credit: Vincenzo Pinto/AFP/Getty Images

Hardcover

ISBN-13: 978-0-8294-4466-7
ISBN-10: 0-8294-4466-1

Paperback

ISBN-13: 978-0-8294-4489-6
ISBN-10: 0-8294-4489-0
Library of Congress Control Number: 2016957586

Printed in the United States of America.
17 18 19 20 21 22 23 Bang 10 9 8 7 6 5 4 3 2 1

The Holy Spirit teaches us: he is the Interior Master. He guides us along the right path, through life's challenges. He teaches us the path, the Way. In the early times of the Church, Christianity was called "the Way" (Acts 9:2), and Jesus himself is the Way. The Holy Spirit teaches us to follow him, to walk in his footprints.

—Homily of Pope Francis, June 8, 2014

CONTENTS

Foreword

Wouldn't you love to take a walk with Pope Francis? In our modern culture, walking has become a great pastime, providing a wonderful opportunity to talk and share. Whether fast-paced or slow and deliberate, walks with another can be great sources of learning, friendship, intimacy, and a renewed spirit.

This collection, which includes excerpts from the homilies and writings of Pope Francis, contributes the content for this walk with him. Picture yourself walking and chatting with Pope Francis along the road. The walk can take many forms. It can be a quick, daily walk, making use of one paragraph from his wise and captivating preaching, or it can be a long walk that takes a chapter at a time.

In many ways, a "walk" embodies the pilgrimage or journey through life. Some walk aimlessly and may even describe their movement as "walking in circles." This walk with Pope Francis is not aimless but proceeds in a precise direction. In fact, it is a walk along "the Way."

In the first two verses of the Acts of the Apostles, chapter 9, the followers of Jesus—those first walkers with Jesus—were said to be followers of "the Way." Here is what the verses say: "Saul, still breathing murderous threats against the disciples of the Lord, asked . . . that, if he should find any men or women who belonged to the Way, he might bring them back to Jerusalem in chains." This passage describes those whom a man named Saul was gathering up for arrest—those known as followers of "the Way." It is very ironic because Saul would soon become the great pilgrim missionary St. Paul, proclaiming "the Way" in virtually every corner of the known world. This book, *Embracing the Way of Jesus*, is about the followers of Jesus, what they saw and believed, and how it changed their lives.

Walks have a way of changing people. In the Christian faith (as in other faiths), the time-honored pilgrimage or procession shapes the mind and heart of the walker. Just as over the centuries walkers have been transformed, so today Jesus continues to transform those who walk with him along "the Way."

The Gospel according to St. Luke, chapter 24, records one such famous walk. The risen Christ comes upon two disciples walking back from Jerusalem to their home in Emmaus. After listening to the woes of these followers, Jesus interprets the Scriptures for them as they walk together. As he explains along the way and then breaks bread with them, their eyes are opened to an encounter with the Lord Jesus, and after he vanishes, they can only say, "Were not our hearts burning within us while he spoke to us on the way and opened the scriptures to us!" So this book can be that companion on the journey, leading the reader more deeply into "the Way" of a follower of Jesus.

This walk with Pope Francis takes one through the Old Testament, the way of the cross, prayer, and other stops along the way, so that those who seek to follow can be encouraged in a new way of seeing, believing, and serving Christ.

Expect to be moved from self-preoccupation into a time of prayer, a prayer that not only refreshes the soul but also opens up new horizons in which you will see both your family and others—the refugee, the "disinherited," our created world—with new eyes and in a new light. Neither nomads wandering aimlessly nor islands cut off from the world, those on "the Way" uncover a dignity in all. "The Way" has that effect of moving the reader along a path to heaven, a path of salvation, given by Jesus himself, who claimed rightly to be the Way, the Truth, and the Life.

There is a charm and a charism to Pope Francis. His words—what he says and the way he says it—have a way of captivating the reader. Perhaps his most distinctive charism is that those who see him from a distance recognize a pastor who wishes to accompany. Like all good pastors, he points to Jesus, who always seems to lead us to surprising stops. Prepare now to join Pope Francis on this walk along "the Way."

Most Reverend Joseph E. Kurtz, DD,
Archbishop of Louisville
April 11, 2016

1

The Way of Discipleship

The apostles, who saw the risen Christ with their own eyes, could not keep silent about their extraordinary experience. He had shown himself to them so that the truth of his resurrection would reach everyone by way of their witness. The Church has the duty to continue this mission over time. Every baptized person is called to bear witness, with his or her life and words, that Jesus is risen, that Jesus is alive and present among us. We are all called to testify that Jesus is alive.

We may ask ourselves: Who is a witness? A witness is a person who has seen [something], who recalls it and tells about it. *See, recall,* and *tell:* these are three verbs that describe the identity and mission. A witness is a person who *has seen* reality with an objective eye but not with an indifferent eye; he has seen and has let himself become involved in the event. For this reason, a person *recalls*, not only because she knows how to reconstruct the events exactly but also because those facts spoke to her and she grasped their profound meaning. Then a witness *tells*, not in a cold and detached way but as one who has allowed himself to be called into question and from that day changed his way of life. A witness is someone who has changed his or her life.

Today all of us are in continuity with that group of apostles who received the Holy Spirit and then went "out" to preach—the Church is sent to take this Gospel message to all people, accompanying it with the signs of the tenderness and power of God. This, too, derives from the event of Pentecost; it is the Holy Spirit, indeed, who overcomes all resistance, to defeat the temptation of our being self-absorbed, [thinking ourselves] among the chosen few, thinking that God's blessing is for us alone. If, for example, some Christians do this and say, "We are the chosen ones, we alone," in the end, they die. They die first spiritually, then they die bodily, because they have no life, they are not capable of generating life, other people, other peoples—they are not apostolic. And it is precisely the Spirit who guides us to meet our brothers and sisters, even those who are most distant in every sense, in order that they may share with us the gifts of love, peace, and joy that the risen Lord has bequeathed us.

Jesus begins his mission not only from a decentralized place but also among men [we would] refer to as having a "low profile." When choosing his first disciples and future apostles, he does not turn to the schools of scribes and doctors of the Law but to humble people and simple people, who diligently prepare for the coming of the Kingdom of God. Jesus goes to call them where they work, on the lakeshore: they are fishermen. He calls them, and they follow him immediately. They leave their nets and go with him; their life will become an extraordinary and fascinating adventure.

The content of Christian witness is not a theory. It's not an ideology or a complex system of precepts and prohibitions or a moralist theory but a message of salvation, a real event. . . . it's a Person: it is the risen Christ, the living and only Savior of all. He can be testified to by those who have personal experience of him, in prayer and in the Church, through a journey that has its foundation in baptism, its nourishment in the Eucharist, its seal in confirmation, its continual conversion in penitence.

But Jesus is present also through the Church, which he sent to extend his mission. Jesus' last message to his disciples is the mandate *to depart*: "Go therefore and make disciples of all nations" (Matt. 28:19). It is a clear mandate, not just an option! The Christian community is a community "going forth," "in departure." More so: the Church was born "going forth." And you will say to me, What about cloistered communities? Yes, these too, for they are always "going forth" through prayer, with the heart open to the world, to the horizons of God. And the elderly, the sick? They, too, [go forth] through prayer and union with the wounds of Jesus.

The Gospel is the word of life. It does not oppress people; on the contrary, it frees those who are slaves to the many evil spirits of this world: the spirit of vanity, attachment to money, pride, sensuality. . . . The Gospel changes the heart, changes life, transforms evil inclinations into good intentions. The Gospel is capable of changing people! Therefore it is the task of Christians to spread the redeeming power throughout the world, becoming missionaries and heralds of the Word of God. This is also suggested by today's passage, which closes with a missionary perspective: "his fame"—the fame of Jesus—"spread everywhere, throughout all the surrounding region of Galilee" (Mark 1:28).

[Galilee] is a borderland, a place of transit where people of different races, cultures, and religions converge. Thus Galilee becomes a symbolic place for the Gospel to open to all nations. From this point of view, Galilee is like the world of today: the co-presence of different cultures [brings] the necessity for comparison and the necessity of encounter. We, too, are immersed every day in a kind of "Galilee of the nations," and in this type of context we may feel afraid and give in to the temptation to build fences to make us feel safer, more protected. But Jesus teaches us that the Good News, which he brings, is not reserved for one part of humanity: it is to be communicated to everyone. It is a proclamation of joy destined for those who are waiting for it, but also for all those who perhaps are no longer waiting for anything and haven't even the strength to seek and to ask.

Starting from Galilee, Jesus teaches us that no one is excluded from the salvation of God; rather, it is from the margins that God prefers to begin, from the least, so as to reach everyone. He teaches us a method, his method, which also expresses the content, which is the Father's mercy. "Each Christian and every community must discern the path that the Lord points out, but all of us are asked to obey his call to go forth from our own comfort zone in order to reach all the 'peripheries' in need of the light of the Gospel" (Apostolic Exhortation, *Evangelii Gaudium*, n. 20).

Jesus calls his disciples and sends them out, giving them clear and precise instructions. He challenges them to take on a whole range of attitudes and ways of acting. Sometimes these can strike us as exaggerated or even absurd.

It would be easier to interpret these attitudes symbolically or "spiritually." But Jesus is quite precise, very clear. He doesn't tell them simply to do whatever they think they can.

Let us think about some of these attitudes: "Take nothing for the journey except a staff; no bread, no bag, no money." "When you enter a house, stay there until you leave the place" (cf. Mark 6:8–11). All this might seem quite unrealistic. We could concentrate on the words *bread, money, bag, staff, sandals,* and *tunic.* And this would be fine. But it strikes me that one key word can easily pass unnoticed among the challenging words I have just listed. It is a word at the heart of Christian spirituality, of our experience of discipleship: *welcome.* Jesus as the good master, the good teacher, sends them out to be welcomed, to experience hospitality. He says to them, "Where you enter a house, stay there." He sends them out to learn one of the hallmarks of the community of believers. We might say that a Christian is someone who has learned to welcome others, who has learned to show hospitality.

Jesus does not send them out as men of influence, landlords, officials armed with rules and regulations. Instead, he makes them see that the Christian journey is simply about changing hearts—one's own heart first [of] all, and then helping to transform the hearts of others. It is about learning to live differently, under a different law, with different rules. It is about turning from the path of selfishness, conflict, division, and superiority, and taking instead the path of life, generosity, and love. It is about passing from a mentality that domineers, stifles, and manipulates to a mentality that welcomes, accepts, and cares.

Jesus sends his disciples out to all nations. To every people. We, too, were part of all those people of two thousand years ago. Jesus did not provide a short list of who is, or is not, worthy of receiving his message and his presence. Instead, he always embraced life as he saw it: in faces of pain, hunger, sickness, and sin; in faces of wounds, of thirst, of weariness, doubt, and pity. Far from expecting a pretty life, smartly dressed and neatly groomed, Jesus embraced life as he found it. It made no difference whether it was dirty, unkempt, broken.

Jesus said, Go out and tell the good news to everyone. Go out and, in my name, embrace life as it is and not as you think it should be. Go out to the highways and byways; go out to tell the good news fearlessly, without prejudice, without superiority, without condescension, to all those who have lost the joy of living. Go out to proclaim the merciful embrace of the Father. Go out to those who are burdened by pain and failure, who feel that their lives are empty, and proclaim the folly of a loving Father who wants to anoint them with the oil of hope, the oil of salvation. Go out to proclaim the good news that error, deceitful illusions, and falsehoods do not have the last word in a person's life. Go out with the ointment that soothes wounds and heals hearts.

All the goods that we have received are to [be given] to others, and thus they increase, as if he were to tell us, "Here is my mercy, my tenderness, my forgiveness; take them and make ample use of them." And what have we done with them? Whom have we "infected" with our faith? How many people have we encouraged with our hope? How much love have we shared with our neighbor? These are questions that will do us good to ask ourselves. Any environment, even the furthest and most impractical, can become a place where our talents can bear fruit. There are no situations or places precluded from the Christian presence and witness. The witness that Jesus asks of us is not closed but is open; it is in our hands.

[We are] not to conceal our faith and our belonging to Christ, not to bury the Word of the Gospel but to let it circulate in our life, in our relationships, in concrete situations, as a strength that galvanizes, purifies, and renews. Similarly, [consider] the forgiveness, which the Lord grants us particularly in the sacrament of reconciliation. Let us not keep it closed within ourselves, but let us allow it to emit its power, which brings down the walls that our egoism has raised, which enables us to take the first step in

> *We are not to conceal our faith and our belonging to Christ, not to bury the Word of the Gospel but to let it circulate in our life, in our relationships, in concrete situations, as a strength that galvanizes, purifies, and renews.*

strained relationships, to resume the dialogue where there is no longer communication.

To his missionary disciples Jesus says, "I am with you always, to the close of the age" (Matt. 28:20). Alone, without Jesus, we can do nothing! In apostolic work, our own strengths, our resources, our structures do not suffice, even if they are necessary. Without the presence of the Lord and the power of his Spirit, our work, though it may be well organized, winds up being ineffective. And thus, we go to tell the nations who Jesus is.

In the voice of Jesus, who tells him, "Come!" [the apostle Peter] recognizes the echo of the first encounter on the shore of that very lake, and right away, once again, he leaves the boat and goes toward the Teacher. And he walks on the waters! The faithful and ready response to the Lord's call always enables one to achieve extraordinary things. But Jesus himself told us that we are capable of performing miracles with our faith—faith in him, faith in his Word, faith in his voice. Peter, however, begins to sink the moment he looks away from Jesus and allows himself to be overwhelmed by the hardships around him. But the Lord is always there, and when Peter calls him, Jesus saves him from danger. Peter's character, with his passion and his weaknesses, can describe our faith: ever fragile and impoverished, anxious yet victorious. Christian faith walks to meet the risen Lord, amidst the world's storms and dangers.

And the final scene is also very important. "And when they got into the boat, the wind ceased. And those in the boat worshipped him, saying, 'Truly you are the Son of God!'" (Matt. 14:32–33). All the disciples are on the boat, united in the experience of weakness, of doubt, of fear, and of "little faith." But when Jesus climbs into that boat again, the weather suddenly changes: they all feel united in their faith in him. All the little and frightened ones become great at the moment in which they fall on their knees and recognize the Son of God in their Teacher. How many times the same thing happens to us! Without Jesus, [when we are] far from Jesus, we feel frightened and inadequate to the point of thinking we cannot succeed. Faith is lacking! But Jesus is always with us, hidden perhaps, but present and ready to support us.

Dear friends, the Lord is calling today, too! The Lord passes through the paths of our daily life. Even today, at this moment, here, the Lord is passing through the square. He is calling us to go with him, to work with him for the Kingdom of God, in the "Galilee" of our times. May each one of you think, *The Lord is passing by today, the Lord is watching me, he is looking at me! What is the Lord saying to me?* And if one of you feels that the Lord says to you, "Follow me," be brave, go with the Lord. The Lord never disappoints. Feel in your heart if the Lord is calling you to follow him. Let's let his gaze rest on us; [may we] hear his voice and follow him! "That the joy of the Gospel may reach to the ends of the earth, illuminating even the fringes of our world."

The Church, the holy People of God, treads the dust-laden paths of history, so often traversed by conflict, injustice, and violence, in order to encounter her children, our brothers and sisters. The holy and faithful People of God are not afraid of losing their way; they are afraid of becoming self-enclosed, frozen into elites, clinging to their own security. They know that self-enclosure, in all the many forms it takes, is the cause of so much apathy. So let us go out, let us go forth to offer everyone the life of Jesus Christ. The People of God can embrace everyone because we are the disciples of the One who knelt before his own to wash their feet.

[On] this journey, ever guided by the Word of God, every Christian can become a witness to the risen Jesus. And his or her witness is all the more credible, the more it shines through a life lived by the Gospel, a joyful, courageous, gentle, peaceful, merciful life. Instead, if a Christian gives in to ease, vanity, and selfishness, if he or she becomes deaf and blind to the question of "resurrection" of many brothers and sisters, how can [that person] communicate the living Jesus? How can the Christian communicate the freeing power of the living Jesus and his infinite tenderness?

Listen to Jesus. He is the Savior: follow him. To listen to Christ, in fact, entails *taking up the logic of his Pascal Mystery*, setting out on the journey with him to make of oneself a gift of love to others, in docile obedience to the will of God, with an attitude of interior freedom and of detachment from worldly things. One must, in other words, be willing to lose one's very life (cf. Mark 8:35), by giving it up so that all men might be saved; thus, we will meet in eternal happiness. The path to Jesus always leads us to happiness—don't forget it! Jesus' way always leads us to happiness. There will always be a cross, trials in the middle, but at the end we are always led to happiness. Jesus does not deceive us; he promised us happiness and will give it to us if we follow his ways.

2

The Holy Spirit Leads Us on the Way

At the baptism, the Holy Spirit descended upon Jesus to *prepare* him for his mission of salvation, the mission of one who is a servant—humble and meek, ready to share and give himself completely. Yet the Holy Spirit, present from the beginning of salvation history, had already been at work in Jesus from the moment of his conception in the virginal womb of Mary of Nazareth, by bringing about the wondrous event of the Incarnation: "The Holy Spirit will come upon you, will overshadow you," the angel said to Mary, "and you will give birth to a son who will be named Jesus" (cf. Luke 1:31, 35–36). The Holy Spirit had then acted in Simeon and Anna on the day of the presentation of Jesus in the Temple (cf. Luke 2:22). Both were awaiting the Messiah, and both were inspired by the Holy Spirit. Simeon and Anna, upon seeing the child, knew immediately that he was the one long awaited by the people.

Then the Holy Spirit descends in the form of a dove: this allows Christ, the Lord's Consecrated One, to inaugurate his mission, which is our salvation. The Holy Spirit: the great One forgotten in our prayers. We often pray to Jesus; we pray to the Father, especially in the Our Father; but we do not often pray to the Holy Spirit—is it true? He is the Forgotten One. And we need to ask for his help, his strength, his inspiration. The Holy Spirit, who has wholly animated the life and mystery of Jesus, is the same Spirit who today guides Christian existence, the existence of men and women who call themselves [Christians] and want to be Christians.

To subject our Christian life and mission, which we have all received in baptism, to the action of the Holy Spirit means finding the apostolic courage necessary to overcome easy worldly accommodations. Christians and communities who are instead deaf to the voice of the Holy Spirit, who urges us to bring the Gospel to the ends of the earth and of society, also become "mutes" who do not speak and do not evangelize.

The Pentecost of the Upper Room in Jerusalem is the beginning, a beginning that endures. The Holy Spirit is the supreme gift of the risen Christ to his apostles, yet he wants that gift to reach everyone. As we read in the Gospel, Jesus says, "I will ask the Father, and he will give you another Advocate to remain with you forever" (John 14:16). It is the Paraclete Spirit, the "Comforter," who grants us the courage to take to the streets of the world, bringing the Gospel! The Holy Spirit makes us look to the horizon and drives us to the very outskirts of existence in order to proclaim life in Jesus Christ.

"As the Father has sent me, even so I send you. . . . Receive the Holy Spirit" (John 20:21–22); this is what Jesus says to us. The [giving] of the Spirit on the evening of the Resurrection took place once again on the day of Pentecost, intensified this time by extraordinary outward signs. On the evening of Easter, Jesus appeared to the apostles and breathed on them his Spirit (cf. John 20:22); on the morning of Pentecost, the outpouring occurred in a resounding way, like a wind that shook the place the apostles were in, filling their minds and hearts. They received a new strength so great that they were able to proclaim Christ's Resurrection in different languages: "They were all filled with the Holy Spirit, and began to speak in other tongues, as the Spirit gave them utterance" (Acts 2:4). Together with them was Mary, the Mother of Jesus, the first disciple, there, too, as Mother of the nascent Church. With her peace, with her smile, with her maternity, she accompanied the joyful young Bride, the Church of Jesus.

As a result, "all of them were filled with the Holy Spirit," who unleashed his irresistible power with amazing consequences: they all "began to speak in different languages, as the Spirit gave them ability." A completely unexpected scene opens up before our eyes: a great crowd gathers, astonished because each one hears the apostles speaking in his own language. They all experience something new, something that had never happened before: "We hear them, each of us, speaking our own language." And what is it that they are speaking about? "God's deeds of power."

This event, which changes the heart and life of the apostles and the other disciples, is immediately felt outside the Upper Room. Indeed, that door kept locked for fifty days is finally thrust open and the first Christian community, no longer closed in upon itself, begins speaking to crowds of different origins about the mighty works that God has done (cf. Acts 2:11)—that is to say, of the resurrection of Jesus, who was crucified. Each one present hears his own language being spoken by the disciples. The gift of the Holy Spirit restores the linguistic harmony that was lost in Babel, prefiguring the universal mission of the apostles.

The Church is not born isolated; she is born universal, one, and catholic, with a precise identity, open to all, not closed, [with] an identity that embraces the entire world, excluding no one. Mother Church closes her door in the face of no one—no one! Not even to the greatest sinner—to no one! This is through the power, through the grace of the Holy Spirit. Mother Church opens . . . wide her doors to everyone because she is Mother.

A fundamental element of Pentecost is *astonishment*. Our God is a God of *astonishment*; this we know. No one expected anything more from the disciples; after Jesus' death, they were a small, insignificant group of defeated orphans of their Master. There occurred instead an unexpected event that astounded: the people were astonished because each of them heard the disciples speaking in their own tongues, telling of the great works of God (Acts 2:6–7, 11).

The Church born at Pentecost is an astounding community because, with the force of her arrival from God, a new message is proclaimed: the resurrection of Christ, with a new language—the universal one of love. A new proclamation: Christ lives, he is risen; a new language: the language of love. The disciples are adorned with power from above and speak with courage. Only minutes before, they all were cowardly, but now they speak with courage and candor, with the freedom of the Holy Spirit.

The Holy Spirit would appear to create disorder in the Church, since he brings the diversity of charisms and gifts. Yet all this, by his working, is a great source of wealth, for the Holy Spirit is the Spirit of unity, which does not mean uniformity but leads everything back to *harmony*. In the Church, it is the Holy Spirit who creates harmony. One of the Fathers of the Church has an expression I love: the Holy Spirit himself is harmony: *Ipse harmonia est.* He is indeed harmony. Only the Spirit can awaken diversity, plurality, and multiplicity, while at the same time building unity. Here, too, when we are the ones who try to create diversity and close ourselves up in what makes us different and other, we bring division. When we are the ones who want to build unity in accordance with our human plans, we end up creating uniformity, standardization.

> *The Church born at Pentecost is an astounding community because, with the force of her arrival from God, a new message is proclaimed: the resurrection of Christ, with a new language—the universal one of love.*

If we let ourselves be guided by the Spirit, [the] richness, variety, and diversity never become sources of conflict because he impels us to experience variety within the communion of the Church. Journeying together in the Church, under the guidance of her pastors who possess a special charism and ministry, is a sign of the Holy Spirit's working. Having a sense of the Church is something fundamental for every Christian, every community, and every movement. It is the Church that brings Christ to me, and me to Christ; parallel journeys are very dangerous! When we venture beyond (*proagon*) the Church's teaching and community—the apostle John tells us in his Second Letter—and do not remain in them, we are not one with the God of Jesus Christ (cf. 2 John 9). So let us ask ourselves, *Am I open to the harmony of the Holy Spirit, overcoming every form of exclusivity? Do I let myself be guided by him, living in the Church and with the Church?*

The Holy Spirit also *anoints*. He anointed Jesus inwardly, and he anoints his disciples so that they can have the mind of Christ and thus be disposed to live lives of peace and communion. Through the anointing of the Spirit, our human nature is sealed with the holiness of Jesus Christ, and we are enabled to love our brothers and sisters with the same love God has for us. We ought, therefore, to show concrete signs of humility, fraternity, forgiveness, and reconciliation. These signs are the prerequisite of a true, stable, and lasting peace. Let us ask the Father to anoint us so that we may fully become his children, ever more conformed to Christ, and may learn to see one another as brothers and sisters. Thus, by putting aside our grievances and divisions, we can show fraternal love for one another. This is what Jesus asks of us in the Gospel: "If you love me, you will keep my commandments. And I will pray the Father, and he will give you another Paraclete, to be with you for ever" (John 14:15–16).

This was the experience of the apostle Paul: "The life I now live in the flesh I live by faith in the Son of God who loved me and gave himself for me" (Gal. 2:20). What is this life? It is God's own life. And who brings us this life? It is the Holy Spirit, the gift of the risen Christ. The Spirit leads us into the divine life as true children of God, as sons and daughters in the only begotten Son, Jesus Christ. Are we open to the Holy Spirit? Do we let ourselves be guided by him? Christians are "spiritual." This does not mean that we are people who live "in the clouds," far removed from real life, as if it were some kind of mirage.

The Christian is someone who thinks and acts in everyday life according to God's will, someone who allows his or her life to be guided and nourished by the Holy Spirit, to be a full life, a life worthy of true sons and daughters. And this entails realism and fruitfulness. Those who let themselves be led by the Holy Spirit are realists: they know how to survey and assess reality. They are also fruitful: their lives bring new life to birth all around them.

The world needs men and women who are not closed in on themselves but filled with the Holy Spirit. Closing oneself off from the Holy Spirit means not only a lack of freedom; it is a sin. There are many ways one can close oneself off to the Holy Spirit: by selfishness for one's own gain; by rigid legalism—seen in the attitude of the doctors of the Law to whom Jesus referred as "hypocrites"; by neglect of what Jesus taught; by living the Christian life not as service to others but in the pursuit of personal interests; and in so many other ways. However, the world needs the courage, hope, faith, and persever-ance of Christ's followers.

In the Christian perspective, a charism is much more than a personal qual-ity, a predisposition that one can be endowed with: a charism is *a grace, a gift bestowed by God the Father, through the action of the Holy Spirit.* And it is a gift that is given to someone not because he is better than others or because he deserves it; it is a gift that God gives him, because with his freely given love he can place him *in service to the entire community,* for the good of all. Speaking in a rather more human way, one says, "God gives this quality, this charism, to this person, not for himself, but in order that he may put it at the service of the whole community."

An important thing that should be highlighted immediately is the fact that *alone, one cannot understand whether one has a charism, and which one.* Many times we have heard someone say, "I have this quality; I can sing really well." And no one has the courage to say, "It's better to keep quiet, because you torture all of us when you sing!" No one can say, "I have this charism." It is within the community that the gifts the Father showers upon us bloom and flourish; and it is *in the bosom of the community* that one learns to recognize them as a sign of [God's] love for all his children.

So each one of us should ask himself or herself, "Is there a charism that the Lord has endowed me with, by the grace of his Spirit, and that my broth-ers and sisters in the Christian community have recognized and encouraged? And how do I act with regard to this gift? Do I use it with generosity, placing it at the service of everyone, or do I overlook it and end up forgetting about it? Or perhaps it becomes a reason for pride in me, such that I always com-plain about others and insist on getting my way in the community?" These are questions we must ask ourselves: if there is a charism in me, if this charism is recognized by the Church, if I am happy with this charism or if I am a bit jealous of the charisms of others, whether I wanted or I want to have that charism. A charism is a gift: God alone bestows it!

The most beautiful experience, though, is the discovery of *all the differ-ent charisms* and all the gifts of his Spirit that the Father showers on his Church! This must not be seen as a reason for confusion, for discomfort;

they are all gifts that God gives to the Christian community in order that it may grow in harmony, in the faith, and in his love, as one body, the Body of Christ. The same Spirit who bestows this diversity of charisms unites the Church. It is always the same Spirit. Before this multitude of charisms, our heart, therefore, must open itself to joy, and we must think, *What a beautiful thing! So many different gifts, because we are all God's children, all loved in a unique way.*

When the Holy Spirit comes to dwell in our hearts, he infuses us with consolation and peace, and he leads us to the awareness of how small we are, with that attitude—strongly recommended by Jesus in the Gospel—of one who places his every care and expectation in God and feels enfolded and sustained by his warmth and protection, just as a child with his father. This is what the Holy Spirit does in our hearts: he makes us feel like children in the arms of our father. In this sense, then, we correctly comprehend how fear of the Lord in us takes on the form of docility, gratitude, and praise, by filling our hearts with hope. Indeed, we frequently fail to grasp the plan of God, and we realize that we are not capable of assuring ourselves of happiness and eternal life. It is precisely in experiencing our own limitations and our poverty, however, that the Holy Spirit comforts us and lets us perceive that the only important thing is to allow ourselves to be led by Jesus into the Father's arms.

The Church is called into being forever, capable of astounding while proclaiming to all that Jesus Christ has conquered death, that God's arms are always open, that his patience is always there awaiting us in order to heal us, to forgive us. The risen Jesus bestowed his Spirit on the Church for this very mission. Take note: if the Church is alive, she must always surprise. It is incumbent upon the living Church to astound. A Church that is unable to astound is a Church that is weak, sick, dying, and that needs admission to the intensive care unit as soon as possible!

As on that day of Pentecost, the Holy Spirit is poured out constantly, even today, on the Church and on each one of us so that we may step outside our mediocrity and our imperviousness and communicate to the entire world the merciful love of the Lord. Communicating the merciful love of the Lord: this is our mission! We, too, have been given the gift of the "tongue" of the Gospel and the "fire" of the Holy Spirit, so that while we proclaim Jesus risen, living and present in our midst, we may warm our heart and also the heart of the peoples drawing near to him [who is] the way, [the] truth, and the life.

3

The Old Testament Way

What is the image we have of God? Perhaps he appears to us as a severe judge, as someone who curtails our freedom and the way we live our lives. But the Scriptures everywhere tell us that God is the Living One, the one who bestows life and points the way to fullness of life. I think of the beginning of the book of Genesis: God fashions man out of the dust of the earth; he breathes in his nostrils the breath of life, and man becomes a living being (cf. Genesis 2:7). *God is the source of life*; thanks to his breath, man has life. God's breath sustains the entire journey of our life on earth.

"And God saw that it was good" (Gen. 1:12, 18, 21, 25). The biblical account of the beginning of the history of the world and of humanity speaks to us of a God who looks at creation, in a sense contemplating it, and declares, "It is good." This, dear brothers and sisters, allows us to enter God's heart and, precisely from within him, to receive his message.

We can ask ourselves: What does this message mean? What does it say to me, to you, to all of us? It says to us simply that this, our world, in the heart and mind of God, is the "house of harmony and peace" and that it is the space in which everyone is able to find their proper place and feel at home because it is "good." All of creation forms a harmonious and good unity, but above all, humanity, made in the image and likeness of God, is one family, in which relationships are marked by a true fraternity not only in words. The other person is a brother or sister to love, and our relationship with God, who is love, fidelity, and goodness, mirrors every human relationship and brings harmony to the whole of creation.

God's world is a world in which everyone feels responsible for the other, for the good of the other. . . . [I]n reflection, fasting, and prayer, each of us deep down should ask ourselves, Is this really the world I desire? Is this really the world we all carry in our hearts? Is the world that we want really a world of harmony and peace, in ourselves, in our relations with others, in families, in cities, *in* and *between* nations? And does not true freedom mean choosing ways in this world that lead to the good of all and are guided by love?

But then we wonder, Is this the world in which we are living? Creation retains its beauty, which fills us with awe, and it remains a good work. But there are also "violence, division, disagreement, war." These occur when man, the summit of creation, stops contemplating beauty and goodness, and withdraws into his own selfishness.

When man thinks only of himself and of his own interests and places himself in the center, when he permits himself to be captivated by the idols of dominion and power, when he puts himself in God's place, then all relationships are broken and everything is ruined; then the door opens to violence, indifference, and conflict. This is precisely what the passage in the book of Genesis seeks to teach us in the story of the Fall: man enters into conflict with himself, he realizes that he is naked and hides himself because he is afraid (Genesis 3:10), he is afraid of God's glance; he accuses the woman, she who is flesh of his flesh (Genesis 3:12); he breaks harmony with creation; he begins to raise his hand against his brother to kill him. Can we say that from harmony he passes to "disharmony"? No, there is no such thing as "disharmony"; there is either harmony or we fall into chaos, where there is violence, argument, conflict, fear.

"Adam, where are you?" "Where is your brother?" These are the two questions that God asks at the dawn of human history and that he also asks each man and woman in our own day—that he also asks us. But I would like us to ask a third question: Has any one of us wept because of this situation [refugees drowning in their attempts to reach Europe] and others like it? Has any one of us grieved for the death of these brothers and sisters? Has any one of us wept for these persons who were on the boat? For the young mothers carrying their babies? For these men who were looking for a means of supporting their families? We are a society that has forgotten how to weep, how to experience compassion—"suffering with" others. The globalization of indifference has taken from us the ability to weep!

It is exactly in this chaos that God asks man's conscience, "Where is Abel your brother?" and Cain responds, "I do not know; am I my brother's keeper?" (Gen. 4:9). We, too, are asked this question. It would be good for us to ask ourselves as well, "Am I really my brother's keeper?" Yes, you are your brother's keeper! To be human means to care for one another! But when harmony is broken, a metamorphosis occurs: the brother who is to be cared for and loved becomes an adversary to fight, to kill. What violence occurs at that moment, how many conflicts, how many wars have marked our history! We need only look at the suffering of so many brothers and sisters.

This is not a question of coincidence but the truth: we bring about the rebirth of Cain in every act of violence and in every war. All of us! And even today we continue this history of conflict between brothers; even today we raise our hands against our brother. Even today we let ourselves be guided by idols, by selfishness, by our own interests, and this attitude persists. We have perfected our weapons, our conscience has fallen asleep, and we have sharpened our ideas to justify ourselves. As if it were normal, we continue to sow destruction, pain, death! Violence and war lead only to death; they speak of death! Violence and war are the language of death!

God chooses Abraham, our father in faith, and asks him to depart, to leave his homeland and set out for another land, which God himself would indicate (Gen. 12:1–9). And in this vocation God did not call Abraham alone, as an individual, but involved from the start his family, his household, and all those in service to his house. . . . God will broaden the horizon still more and will shower Abraham with his blessing, promising him descendants as numerous as the stars in the sky and as grains of sand on the shore. The first important date is precisely this: Starting from Abraham, God forms a people to carry his blessing to all the families of the earth. And it is within this people that Jesus is born. It is God who fashions this people, this history, the journeying Church, and there Jesus is born, [among] this people.

Abraham and his own listen to the call of God and set out on the journey, despite not knowing well who this God is and where he wants to lead them. It's true, because Abraham sets out on the journey entrusting himself to this God who spoke to him, yet he has no theology book to study what this God might be. He trusts; he trusts in love. God makes him feel

Abraham and his own listen to the call of God and set out on the journey, despite not knowing well who this God is and where he wants to lead them.

love, and Abraham trusts. This, however, does not mean that the people are always firm and faithful. Indeed, from the outset there is resistance, retreating into themselves and their own interests and the temptation to bargain with God and resolve matters in their own way. And these are the betrayals and sins that mark the journey of the people throughout all of salvation history, which is *the history of the faithfulness of God and the infidelity of his people.* God, however, does not tire; God has patience. He has a great deal of patience and in time continues to educate and to form his people, as a father with his own child. God walks with us.

Walking. This verb makes us reflect on the course of history, that long journey that is the history of salvation, starting with Abraham, our father in faith, whom the Lord called one day to set out, to go forth from his country toward the land that God would show him. From that time on, our identity as believers has been that of a people making its pilgrim way toward the Promised Land. This history has always been accompanied by the Lord! He is ever faithful to his covenant and to his promises. Because he is faithful, "God is light, and in him there is no darkness at all" (1 John 1:5). Yet on the part of the people there are times of both light and darkness, fidelity and infidelity, obedience and rebellion—times of being a pilgrim people and times of being a people adrift.

[In] the calling of Moses . . . the Lord says that he is the God of Abraham, the God of Isaac, and the God of Jacob, the God of the living. When he sends Moses to Pharaoh to set his people free, he reveals his name: "I am who I am," the God who enters our history, sets us free from slavery and death, and brings life to his people because he is the Living One. I also think of the gift of the Ten Commandments: a path God points out to us toward a life that is truly free and fulfilling. The commandments are not a litany of prohibitions—you must not do this, you must not do that, you must not do the other; on the contrary, they are a great "Yes!": a yes to God, to love, to life. Dear friends, our lives are fulfilled in God alone, because only he is the Living One!

[This is] the ancient prayer of blessing that God gave to Moses to hand on to Aaron and his sons: "The Lord bless you and keep you. The Lord make his face to shine upon you, and be gracious to you. The Lord lift up his countenance upon you and give you peace" (Num. 6:24–25). There is no more meaningful time than the beginning of a new year to hear these words of blessing. They will accompany our journey through the year, opening up before us. They are words of strength, courage, and hope. Not an illusory hope, based on frail human promises, or a naive hope that presumes that the future will be better simply because it is the future. Rather, it is a hope that has its foundation precisely in God's blessing, a blessing that contains the greatest message of good wishes there can be. And this is the message the Church brings to each of us, filled with the Lord's loving care and providential help.

"The Lord your God . . . fed you with manna, which you did not know" (Deut. 8:2–3). These words from Deuteronomy make reference to the history of the Israelites, whom God led out of Egypt, out of slavery, and for forty years led through the desert toward the Promised Land. Once established on the land, the Chosen People attain a certain autonomy, a certain well-being, and run *the risk of forgetting* the harrowing events of the past, overcome [with] thanks for God's intervention and for his infinite goodness. And so the Scriptures urge the people to recall, to remember, *to memorize*, the entire walk through the desert, in times of famine and desperation. The command of Moses is to return to the basics, to the experience of total dependence on God, when survival was placed in his hands, so the people would understand that "man does not live by bread alone, but that man lives by everything that proceeds out of the mouth of the Lord" (Deut. 8:3).

The prophet Hosea says, "I have walked with you, and I taught you how to walk as a father teaches his child to walk" (cf. Hosea 11:3–4). It's beautiful, this image of God! And this is God with us: he teaches us to walk. And it is the same attitude he maintains toward the Church. We, too, despite our resolve to follow the Lord Jesus, experience every day the selfishness and hardness of our heart. When, however, we recognize ourselves as sinners, God fills us with his mercy and with his love. And he forgives us; he always forgives us. And it is precisely this that makes us grow as God's people, as the Church: not our cleverness, not our merits—we are a small thing, it's not that—but the daily experience of how much the Lord wishes us well and takes care of us. It is this that makes us feel that we are truly his, in his hands, and makes us grow in communion with him and with one another.

Dear friends, this is God's plan; when he called Abraham, God was thinking of this: to form people blessed in his love and that they might carry his blessing to all nations of the earth. This plan does not change; it is always in action. In Christ it found fulfillment, and today, still, God continues to realize it in the Church. Let us ask, then, for the grace to remain faithful to following the Lord Jesus and to listening to his Word, ready to set out every day, like Abraham, toward the land of God and of man, our true homeland, and thus to become the blessing, the sign of God's love for all his children. I like to think that a synonym, another name that we Christians could be called, is this: we are men and women, we are a people who bless. The Christian by his life must bless always—bless God and bless all people. We Christians are a people who bless, who know how to bless.

"The people who walked in darkness have seen a great light" (Isa. 9:2). This prophecy of Isaiah never ceases to touch us. . . . This is not simply an emotional or sentimental matter. It moves us because it states the deep reality of what we are: a people who walk, [while] all around us—and within us as well—there is darkness and light. In this night, as the spirit of darkness enfolds the world, there takes place anew the event that always amazes and surprises us: the people who walk see a great light. A light that makes us reflect on this mystery: the mystery of *walking* and *seeing*.

The prophet Isaiah is addressing a people who have been through a dark period of exile, a very difficult trial. But now the time of consolation has come for Jerusalem; sadness and fear must give way to joy: "Rejoice . . . be glad . . . rejoice with her in joy," says the prophet (Isa. 66:10). It is a great invitation to joy. Why? What is the reason for this invitation to joy? Because the Lord is going to pour out over the Holy City and its inhabitants a cascade of consolation, a veritable overflow of consolation—such that it will be over-come—a cascade of maternal tenderness: "You shall be carried upon her hip and dandled upon her knees" (verse 12). As when a mother takes her child upon her knee and caresses him or her, so the Lord will do and does with us. This is the cascade of tenderness that gives us much consolation: "As one whom his mother comforts, so I will comfort you" (verse 13).

Every Christian, and especially you or I, is called to be a bearer of this message of hope that gives serenity and joy: God's consolation, his tenderness toward all. But if we first experience the joy of being consoled by him, of being loved by him, then we can bring that joy to others. This is important if our mission is to be fruitful: to feel God's consolation and to pass it on to others! . . . The Lord is a Father, and he says that he will be for us like a mother with her baby, with a mother's tenderness. Do not be afraid of the consolations of the Lord. Isaiah's invitation must resound in our hearts: "Comfort, comfort my people" (Isa. 40:1), and this must lead to mission. We must find the Lord who consoles us and go to console the people of God. This is the mission. People today certainly need words, but most of all they need us to bear witness to the mercy and tenderness of the Lord, which warm the heart, rekindle hope, and attract people toward the good. What a joy it is to bring God's consolation to others!

4

The Way of the Cross

Jesus pronounces a prophecy that reveals his identity and shows the path to know him truly: "The hour has come for the Son of Man to be glorified" (John 12:23). It is *the hour of the Cross!* It is the time for the defeat of Satan, prince of evil, and for the definitive triumph of the merciful love of God. Christ declares that he will be "lifted up from the earth" (John 12:32), an expression with a twofold meaning: "lifted" because he is crucified and "lifted" because he is exalted by the Father in the Resurrection, to draw everyone to him and to reconcile mankind with God and among themselves. The hour of the Cross, the darkest in history, is also the source of salvation for those who believe in him.

The same Peter who professed Jesus Christ now says to him [in essence], "You are the Christ, the Son of the living God. I will follow you, but let us not speak of the Cross. That has nothing to do with it. I will follow you on other terms, but without the Cross." When we journey without the Cross, when we build without the Cross, when we profess Christ without the Cross, we are not disciples of the Lord, we are worldly. We may be bishops, priests, cardinals, popes, [laity], but not disciples of the Lord.

According to an ancient Roman tradition, while fleeing the city during the persecutions of Nero, Saint Peter saw Jesus, who was travelling in the opposite direction—that is, toward the city, and asked him in amazement, "Lord, where are you going?" Jesus' response was, "I am going to Rome to be crucified again." At that moment, Peter understood that he had to follow the Lord with courage, to the very end. But he also realized that he would never be alone on the journey; Jesus, who had loved him even unto death, would always be with him. Jesus, with his Cross, walks with us and takes upon himself our fears, our problems, and our sufferings, even those that are deepest and most painful. With the Cross, Jesus unites himself to the silence of the victims of violence, those who can no longer cry out, especially the innocent and the defenseless. With the Cross, he is united to families in trouble, and those who mourn the tragic loss of their children.

To those who, today too, wish to see Jesus, to those who are searching for the face of God, to those who received catechesis when they were little and then developed it no further and perhaps have lost their faith, to so many who have not yet encountered Jesus personally . . . to all these people we can offer three things: *the Gospel, the crucifix, and the witness* of our faith, poor but sincere. The Gospel: there we can encounter Jesus, listen to him, know him. The Crucifix: the sign of the love of Jesus, who gave himself for us. And then a faith that is expressed in simple gestures of fraternal charity. But mainly in the coherence of life, between what we say and what we do. Coherence between our faith and our life, between our words and our actions: Gospel, crucifix, witness.

The Gospel presents the episode of the expulsion of the merchants from the temple (John 2:13–25). Jesus made "a whip of cords, he drove them all, with the sheep and oxen, out of the temple" (John 2:15)—the money, everything. Such a gesture gave rise to strong impressions in the people and in the disciples. It clearly appeared as *a prophetic gesture*, so much so that some of those present asked Jesus, "What sign have you to show us for doing this?" (John 2:18), and "Who are you to do these things? Show us a sign that you have authority to do them."

They were seeking a divine and prodigious sign that would confirm that Jesus was sent by God. And he responded, "Destroy this temple, and in three days I will raise it up" (John 2:19). They replied, "It has taken 46 years to build this temple, and you will raise it up in three days?" (John 2:20). They did not understand that the Lord was referring to the *living temple of his body* that would be destroyed in the death on the Cross but would be raised on the third day. Thus, in three days. "When therefore he was raised from the dead, his disciples remembered that he had said this; and they believed the Scripture and the word Jesus had spoken" (John 2:22).

God placed on Jesus' Cross all the weight of our sins, all the injustices perpetrated by every Cain against his brother, all the bitterness of the betrayal by Judas and by Peter, all the vanity of tyrants, all the arrogance of false friends. It was a heavy Cross, like night experienced by abandoned people, heavy like the death of loved ones, heavy because it carries all the ugliness of evil. However, the Cross is also glorious like the

> *The Cross is also glorious like the dawn after a long night, for it represents all the love of God, which is greater than our iniquities and our betrayals.*

dawn after a long night, for it represents all the love of God, which is greater than our iniquities and our betrayals. In the Cross we see the monstrosity of man, when he allows evil to guide him; but we also see the immensity of the mercy of God, who does not treat us according to our sins but according to his mercy.

Jesus is united with every person who suffers from hunger in a world that . . . permits itself the luxury of throwing away tons of food every day. On the Cross, Jesus is united to the many mothers and fathers who suffer as they see their children become victims of drug-induced euphoria. On the Cross, Jesus is united with those who are persecuted for their religion, for their beliefs, or simply for the color of their skin. On the Cross, Jesus is united with so many young people who have lost faith in political institutions because they see in them only selfishness and corruption; he unites himself with those young people who have lost faith in the Church or even in God because of the counter-witness of Christians and ministers of the Gospel.

How our inconsistencies make Jesus suffer! The Cross of Christ bears the suffering and the sin of [humanity], including our own. Jesus accepts all this with open arms, bearing on his shoulders our crosses and saying to us, "Have courage! You do not carry your cross alone! I carry it with you. I have overcome death, and I have come to give you hope, to give you life" (cf. John 3:16).

Do you want to be like Pilate, who did not have the courage to go against the tide to save Jesus' life, and instead washed his hands? Tell me: are you one of those who wash their hands, who feign ignorance and look the other way? Or are you like Simon of Cyrene, who helped Jesus carry that heavy wood, or like Mary and the other women, who were not afraid to accompany Jesus all the way to the end, with love and tenderness? And you, who do you want to be? Like Pilate? Like Simon? Like Mary? Jesus is looking at you now and is asking you: do you want to help me carry the Cross? Brothers and sisters . . . how will you respond to him?

Again, the Gospel offers us the words that Jesus addressed to Nicodemus: "For God so loved the world that he gave his only Son" (John 3:16). In hearing these words, we turn our heart's gaze to Jesus crucified, and we feel within us that God loves us, truly loves us, and he loves us so much! This is the simplest expression that epitomizes all the Gospel, all the faith, all theology: *God loves us with a free and boundless love.*

According to the evangelist John, the first proclamation of the death and resurrection of Christ: Christ's body, destroyed on the Cross by the violence of sin, *will become in the Resurrection the universal meeting place between God and humankind.* And the risen Christ is himself the universal meeting place—for everyone!—between God and humankind. For this reason, his humanity is the true temple where God is revealed, speaks, is encountered. And the *true worshippers*, the true worshippers of God are not only the guardians of the material temple, the keepers of power and of religious knowledge [but] they are [also] those who *worship God "in spirit and truth"* (John 4:23).

While we contemplate and celebrate the Holy Cross, we think, with emotion, of so many of our brothers and sisters who are being persecuted and killed because of their faith in Christ. This happens especially wherever religious freedom is still not guaranteed or fully realized. It happens, however, even in countries and areas that, in principle, protect freedom and human rights but where, in practice, believers, and especially Christians, encounter restrictions and discrimination. So . . . we remember them and pray for them in a special way.

Let us walk in the world as Jesus did, and let us make our whole existence a sign of our love for our brothers, especially the weakest and poorest. *Let us build for God a temple of our lives.* And so we make it "encounterable" for those we find along our journey. If we are witnesses of the Living Christ, so many people will encounter Jesus in us, in our witness. But, we ask—and each one of us can ask ourselves—does the Lord feel at home in my life? Do we allow him to "cleanse" our hearts and to drive out the idols, those attitudes of cupidity, jealousy, worldliness, envy, hatred, those habits of gossiping and tearing down others? Do [we] allow him to cleanse all the behaviors that are against God, against our neighbor, and against ourselves? . . . . Each one can answer for him- or herself, in the silence of [the] heart: "Do I allow Jesus to make my heart a little cleaner?" "Oh Father, I fear the rod!"

But Jesus never strikes [us]. Jesus cleanses with tenderness, mercy, and love. Mercy is his way of cleansing. Let us, each of us, allow the Lord to enter with his mercy—not with the whip, no, with his mercy—to cleanse our hearts. With us, Jesus' whip is his mercy. Let us open to him the gates so that he will make us a little purer.

Why was the Cross necessary? Because of the gravity of the evil that enslaved us. The Cross of Jesus expresses all the negative forces of evil but, also, all the gentle omnipotence of God's mercy. The Cross would seem to decree Christ's failure, but in reality it signals his victory. On Calvary, those who mocked him said to him, "If you are the Son of God, come down from the cross" (Matt. 27:40). But the opposite was true: it was precisely because Jesus was the Son of God that he was there, on the Cross, faithful to the end to the loving plan of the Father. And for this very reason God "exalted" Jesus (Phil. 2:9), conferring universal kingship on him.

When we look to the Cross where Jesus was nailed, we contemplate the sign of love, of the infinite love of God for each of us and the source of our salvation. The mercy of God, which embraces the whole world, springs from the Cross. Through the Cross of Christ, the evil one is overcome, death is defeated, life is given to us, [and] hope is restored. This is important: through the Cross of Christ, hope is restored to us. The Cross of Jesus is our one true hope! That is why the Church "exalts" the Holy Cross and why we

Christians bless ourselves with the sign of the cross. That is, we don't exalt crosses [in general] but [do exalt] the glorious Cross of Christ, the sign of God's immense love, the sign of our salvation and path toward the resurrection. This is our hope.

Before the Cross of Jesus, we apprehend in a way that we can almost touch with our hands how much we are eternally loved; before the Cross we feel that we are children and not things or objects, as St. Gregory of Nazianzus says, addressing Christ with this prayer: "Were it not for You, O my Christ, I would feel like a finite creature. I was born and I feel myself dissolve. I eat, I sleep, I rest and I walk, I fall ill and I recover. Longings and torments without number assail me; I enjoy the sun and how the earth bears fruit. Then, I die and my flesh turns to dust just like that of animals, who have not sinned. But what have I more than them? Nothing, if not God. Were it not for you, O Christ mine, I would feel myself a lost creature. O, Our Jesus, guide us from the Cross to the resurrection and teach us that evil shall not have the last word, but love, mercy, and forgiveness. O Christ, help us to exclaim again, 'Yesterday I was crucified with Christ; today I am glorified with Him. Yesterday I died with Him; today I live with Him. Yesterday I was buried with Him; today I am raised with Him.'"

On Calvary, there at the foot of the Cross, was the Virgin Mary (cf. John 19:25–27). She is Our Lady of Sorrows. To her I entrust the present and the future of the Church, so that we may all always be able to discover and welcome the message of love and salvation of the Cross of Christ.

St. Paul reminds us, "God, who is rich in mercy"—never forget that he is rich in mercy—"out of the great love with which he loved us, even when we were dead through our trespasses, made us alive together with Christ" (Eph. 2:5). The *Cross of Christ* is the supreme proof of the mercy and love that God has for us: Jesus loved us *"to the end"* (John 13:1), meaning not only to the last instant of his earthly life but also to the farthest limit of love. While in creation the Father gave us proof of his immense love by giving us life, in the passion and death of his Son he gave us the proof of proofs: he came to suffer and die for us. So great is God's mercy: he loves us, he forgives us. God forgives all and God forgives always.

The Cross is the word through which God has responded to evil in the world. Sometimes it may seem as though God does not react to evil, as if he is silent. And yet, God has spoken, he has replied, and his answer is the Cross of Christ: a word that is love, mercy, forgiveness. It also reveals a judgment, namely that God, in judging us, loves us. Let us remember this: God judges us by loving us. If I embrace his love, then I am saved; if I refuse it, then I am condemned, not by him, but [by] my own self, because God never condemns, he only loves and saves.

Impress, Lord, in our hearts the sentiments of faith, hope, love, and sorrow for our sins. Lead us to repent for our sins, which crucified you. Lead us to transform our conversion made up of words into a conversion of life and deeds. Lead us to guard within us the living memory of your disfigured face, so as never to forget the terrible price you paid for our freedom.

Jesus Crucified, strengthen faith in us so that we do not fall in the face of temptation; revive hope in us so that we do not go astray toward the seductions of the world; guard charity in us so that we are not fooled by corruption and worldliness. Teach us that the Cross is the way to the resurrection. Teach us that Good Friday is the road to an Easter of light. Teach us that God never forgets a single one of his children and never tires of forgiving us and embracing us with his infinite mercy. Teach us, also, to never tire of asking for forgiveness, of believing in the boundless mercy of the Father.

The Cross of Christ contains all the love of God; there we find his immeasurable mercy. This is a love in which we can place all our trust, in which we can believe. . . . Let us entrust ourselves to Jesus, let us give ourselves over to him, because he never disappoints anyone! Only in Christ crucified and risen can we find salvation and redemption. With him, evil, suffering, and death do not have the last word, because he gives us hope and life: he has transformed the Cross from being an instrument of hate, defeat, and death to being a sign of love, victory, triumph, and life.

5

The Way of Christian Worship

[May we worship] him! The book of Revelation speaks to us of worship: the myriads of angels, all creatures, the living beings, the elders, prostrate themselves before the Throne of God and of the Lamb that was slain, namely Christ, to whom be praise, honor and glory (cf. Rev. 5:11–14). I would like all of us to ask ourselves this question: [Do] we worship the Lord? Do we turn to God only to ask him for things, to thank him, or do we also turn to him to worship him?

What does it mean, then, to worship God? It means learning to be with him, it means that we stop trying to dialogue with him, and it means sensing that his presence is the truest, the best, the most important thing of all. All of us, in our own lives, consciously and perhaps sometimes unconsciously, have a very clear order of priority concerning the things we consider important. Worshipping the Lord means giving him the place that he must have; worshipping the Lord means stating, believing—not only by our words—that he alone truly guides our lives; worshipping the Lord means that we are convinced before him that he is the only God, the God of our lives, the God of our history.

The woman [at the well] asks Jesus about the place where God is truly worshipped. Jesus does not side with the mountain or the temple but goes deeper. He goes to the heart of the matter, breaking down every wall of division. He speaks instead of the meaning of true worship: "God is spirit, and those who worship him must worship in spirit and truth" (John 4:24). So many past controversies between Christians can be overcome when we put aside all polemical or apologetic approaches and seek instead to grasp more fully what unites us, namely, our call to share in the mystery of the Father's love revealed to us by the Son through the Holy Spirit.

We have to empty ourselves of the many small or great idols that we have and in which we take refuge, on which we often seek to base our security. They are idols that we sometimes keep well hidden; they can be ambition, careerism, a taste for success, placing ourselves at the center, the tendency to dominate others, the claim to be the sole masters of our lives, some sins to which we are bound, and many others. . . . I would like a question to resound in the heart of each one of you, and I would like you to answer it honestly: "Have I considered which idol lies hidden in my life that prevents me from worshipping the Lord?" Worshipping is stripping ourselves of our idols, even the most hidden ones, and choosing the Lord as the center, as the highway of our lives.

[On the feast of Corpus Christi] the Church praises the Lord for the gift of the Eucharist. While on Holy Thursday we commemorate its institution at the Last Supper, Corpus Christi is for giving thanks and adoration. And in fact, there is a traditional procession with the Most Holy Sacrament on this day. *To adore Eucharistic Jesus and to walk with him.* These are the two insep-arable aspects of the feast, two aspects that characterize the entire life of the Christian people: a people who adore God and a people who walk, who do not stand still but who journey!

First of all we are *a people who adore God*. We adore God who is love, who in Jesus Christ gave himself for us, offered himself on the Cross to atone for our sins, and by the power of this love rose from the dead and lives in his Church. We have no other God but he!

Let us confess . . . as we turn our gaze to the Corpus Christi, the Sacra-ment on the altar. And by this faith, we renounce Satan and all his machina-tions; we renounce the idols of money, vanity, pride, power, and violence. We Christians don't want to worship anything and anyone in this world except for Jesus Christ, who is present in the Holy Eucharist. Perhaps we don't always understand the full meaning of our profession of faith, what conse-quences it has or should have.

Our faith in the true presence of Jesus Christ, true God and true Man, in the consecrated Bread and Wine, is authentic if we commit ourselves to *walk behind him and with him*. To adore and to walk: a people who adore are a people who walk! Walk with him and behind him, as we seek to practice *his* commandment, the one he gave the disciples precisely at the Last Supper: "Even as I have loved you, that you also love one another" (John 13:34). People who adore God in the Eucharist are people who walk in charity. To adore God in the Eucharist [is] to walk with God in fraternal charity.

The Lord Jesus never ceases to inspire acts of charity in his people journeying along the path! . . . You [who are young], let no one steal your hope! I've said it many times, and I will repeat it once more: don't let them steal your hope! Adoring Jesus in your hearts and staying united with him, you will know how to stand up to evil, to injustice, and to violence with the strength of goodness, honesty, and virtue.

Dear brothers and sisters, the Eucharist has brought you together. The Body of the Lord makes us a single thing, a single family, the People of God reunited around Jesus, the Bread of life. What I told the young people I say to everyone: if you adore Christ and walk behind him and with him, your diocesan church and your parishes will grow in faith and in charity, in the joy of evangelizing. You'll be a Church in which fathers, mothers, priests, men and women religious, catechists, children, old and young people walk alongside one another, support one another, help one another, love one another like brothers and sisters, especially in difficult times.

Christian unity—we are convinced—will not be the fruit of subtle theoretical discussions in which each party tries to convince the other of the soundness of their opinions. When the Son of Man comes, he will find us still discussing! We need to realize that to plumb the depths of the mystery of God, we need one another, we need to encounter one another and to challenge one another under the guidance of the Holy Spirit, who harmonizes diversities, overcomes conflicts, and reconciles differences.

On the occasion of the Jewish Passover, Jesus goes to Jerusalem. When he arrives at the temple, he does not find people seeking God but people conducting business: merchants of livestock for sacrificial offerings; money changers who exchange the "impure" money bearing the emperor's image with coins approved by the religious authority in order to pay the annual temple fee. What do we find when we go, when we go to our temples? I'll leave this question. Ignoble trade, a source of lavish earnings, provokes a forceful response from Jesus. He overturns the tables and throws the money to the ground and sends the merchants away, telling them, "You shall not make my Father's house a house of trade!" (John 2:16). This expression does not merely refer to the dealings in the temple courtyards. It instead refers to a type of religiosity.

This act of Jesus *is an act of cleansing, of purification*, and the attitude he renounces can be gleaned from the prophetic texts, according to which God does not appreciate exterior worship performed with material sacrifices and based on personal interests (cf. Isa. 1:11–17; Jer. 7:2–11). This act is a reference to authentic worship, to a correspondence between liturgy and life, an appeal that applies in every age and even for us today—that correspondence between liturgy and life. The liturgy is not something unusual, over there, far away, and while celebrating I think about many things or I pray the rosary. No, no. There is a correspondence with the liturgical celebration, which we then carry in our life; and we must always persevere in this; we still have a long way to go.

The liturgy [is] "the primary and indispensable source from which the faithful are to derive the true Christian spirit." This means reaffirming the essential bond that unites the life of a disciple of Jesus with liturgical worship. This is not primarily a doctrine to be understood or a rite to be performed; naturally it is also this, but in another way, it is essentially different: it is a font of life and of light for our pilgrimage of faith.

> *The Church calls us to have and to foster an authentic liturgical life, so that there may be harmony between that which the liturgy celebrates and that which we experience in our lives.*

Therefore, the Church calls us to have and to foster an authentic liturgical life, so that there may be harmony between that which the liturgy celebrates and that which we experience in our lives. It means expressing in life what we have received through the faith and how much we have celebrated here.

[Our liturgy] is about fulfilling an itinerary of conversion and atonement, to remove the remnants of sin, as Jesus did, cleansing the temple of wretched interests. *Lent is the appropriate time for all of this; it is the time of inner renewal,* of the remission of sins, the time at which we are called to rediscover the sacrament of penance and reconciliation, which lets us pass from the shadows of sin to the light of grace and of friendship with Jesus. The great power this sacrament has in Christian life must not be forgotten. It enables us to grow in union with God and lets us reacquire lost joy and experience the comfort of feeling personally held in God's merciful embrace.

A disciple of Jesus does not go to church simply to observe a precept, to feel that he or she is in good standing with God who then will not "disturb" the person too much. "But Lord, I go every Sunday, I do. . . . Don't interfere in my life, don't disturb me." This is the attitude of so many Catholics, so many. A disciple of Jesus goes to church to encounter the Lord and to find in his grace, operating in the sacraments, the power to think and act according to the Gospel. This is why we cannot mislead ourselves that we are able to enter the Lord's house and "cover up," with prayer and acts of devotion, conduct contrary to the requirements of justice, honesty, and charity to our neighbor. We cannot substitute with "religious tributes" what is owed to our neighbor, postponing true conversion. Worship, liturgical celebrations, [form] the privileged setting [in which] to hear the voice of the Lord, who guides us on the path of rectitude and Christian perfection.

The prayer of praise is a Christian prayer, for all of us. In the Mass, every day, when we sing the "Holy, Holy, Holy," this is a prayer of praise: we praise God for his greatness because he is great. And we address him with beautiful words because it pleases us to do this. The prayer of praise bears fruit in us. Sarah danced as she celebrated her fertility—at the age of ninety! This fruitfulness gives praise to God. Men and women who praise the Lord, who pray praising the Lord—and who are happy to do so—rejoice in singing the *Sanctus* at Mass, and they bear fruit. Let us consider how beautiful it is to offer the prayer of praise to God. This should be our prayer and, as we offer it up to God, we ought to say to ourselves, "Arise, O heart, because you are standing before the King of Glory."

Together with the prayer of praise, the prayer of intercession is, in these days, a cry to the Father for our Christian brothers and sisters who are persecuted and murdered, and for the cause of peace in our turbulent world. Praise the Lord at all times; never cease to do so; praise him more and more, unceasingly. I have been told of Charismatic prayer groups in which they pray the rosary. Prayer to the Mother of God must never be excluded, never! But when you assemble for prayer, praise the Lord!

This relationship with the Lord is . . . a bond that comes from within. It is *a relationship lived with the heart*: it is our friendship with God, granted to us by Jesus, a friendship that changes our life and fills us with passion, with joy. Thus, the gift of piety stirs in us, above all, gratitude and praise. This is, in fact, the reason and *the most authentic meaning of our worship and our adoration*. When the Holy Spirit allows us to perceive the presence of the Lord and all his love for us, it warms the heart and moves us quite naturally to prayer and celebration. Piety, therefore, is synonymous with the genuine religious spirit, with filial trust in God, with that capacity to pray to him with the love and simplicity that belong to those who are humble of heart.

In the Letter to the Romans the apostle Paul states, "For all who are led by the Spirit of God are sons of God. For you did not receive the spirit of slavery to fall back into fear, but you have received the spirit of sonship," from which, "we cry, 'Abba! Father!'" (Rom. 8:14–15). Let us ask the Lord for the gift of his Spirit to conquer our fear, our uncertainty, and our restless, impatient spirit, and to make of us joyful witnesses of God and of his love by worshipping the Lord in truth and in service to our neighbor with gentleness and with a smile, which the Holy Spirit always gives us in joy. May the Holy Spirit grant to all of us this gift of piety.

Prayer expresses what we experience and what we ought to experience in our daily lives. At least that is true of prayer that is not self-centered or merely for show. Prayer makes us put into practice, or examine our consciences about, what we have prayed for in the Psalms. We are the hands of God, who "lifts up the poor from the dust" (Psalm 113:7). We work to turn what is dry and barren into the joy of fertile ground. We cry out that "precious in the eyes of the Lord is the life of his faithful ones." We are those who fight, speak up, and defend the dignity of every human life, from conception to old age, when our years are many and our strength fails.

Prayer is the reflection of our love for God, for others, and for all creation. The commandment of love is the greatest way for the missionary disciple to be conformed to Jesus. Union with Jesus deepens our Christian vocation, which is concerned with what Jesus "does"—which is something much greater than mere "activities"—with becoming more like him in all that we do. The beauty of the ecclesial community is born of this union of each of her members to the person of Jesus, creating an "ensemble of vocations" in the richness of harmonic diversity.

If the gift of piety makes us grow in relation to and in communion with God and leads us to live as his children, at the same time, it helps us *to pass this love on to others as well and to recognize them as our brothers and sisters.* And then, yes, we will be moved by feelings of piety—not pietism!—in relation to those around us and to those we encounter every day. Why do I say "not pietism"? Because some think that to be pious is to close one's eyes, to pose like a picture, and pretend to be a saint. In Piedmont we say: to play the "mugna quacia" [literally: the pious or serene nun]. This is not the gift of piety.

The gift of piety means to be truly capable of rejoicing with those who rejoice, of weeping with those who weep, of being close to those who are lonely or in anguish, of correcting those in error, of consoling the afflicted, of welcoming and helping those in need. The gift of piety is closely tied to gentleness. The gift of piety, which the Holy Spirit gives us, makes us gentle, makes us calm, patient, at peace with God, at the service of others with gentleness.

6

The Way of Prayer

It is not Abraham who builds about himself a people, but God who gives life to this people. Usually it was man who turned to the divinity, seeking to bridge the gap and invoking aid and protection. The people prayed to gods, divinities. In this case, however, something unheard of happens: it is God himself who takes the initiative. Let us hear this: it is God himself who knocks at Abraham's door and says to him, Go forth, leave your land, begin to walk, and I will make of you a great people. And this is the beginning of the Church, and within this people Jesus is born. God takes the initiative and turns his word [in]to man, creating a bond and a new relationship with him. "But, Father, how can this be? God speaks to us?" "Yes." "And we can speak to God?" "Yes." "But can we have a conversation with God?" "Yes." This is called prayer, but it is God who started it all.

God forms a people with all those who listen to his Word and set themselves on the journey, trusting in him. This is the only condition: to trust in God. If you trust in God, listen to him, and set out on the journey, this is building the Church. The love of God *precedes* everything. God is always first, he arrives before us, he precedes us. The prophet Jeremiah (1:11) said that God is like an almond blossom, because it is the first tree to flower in spring. Meaning that God always flowers before us.

When we arrive, God is waiting for us, he calls us, he makes us walk. Always anticipating us. And this is called love, because God always waits for us. "But, Father, I don't believe this, because if you only knew, Father; my life was so horrible, how can I think that God is waiting for me?" God is waiting for you. And if you were a great sinner, he is waiting for you even more and waiting for you with great love, because he is first. This is the beauty of the Church, who leads us to this God who is waiting for us! He precedes Abraham, he precedes even Adam.

We become accustomed to living in a society that thinks it can do without God, in which parents no longer teach their children to pray or to make the sign of the Cross. I ask you: do your children, do your little ones know how to make the sign of the Cross? Think about it. Do your grandchildren know how to make the sign of the Cross? Have you taught them? Think about it and respond in your heart. Do they know how to pray the Our Father? Do they know how to pray to Our Lady with the Hail Mary? Think about it and respond within yourselves. Growing accustomed to unchristian and convenient behavior narcotizes the heart!

The family prays. The Gospel passage Luke 18:9–14 speaks about two ways of praying. That of the Pharisee is false, and that of the tax collector is authentic. The Pharisee embodies an attitude that does not express thanksgiving to God for his blessings and his mercy, but, rather, [expresses] self-satisfaction. The Pharisee feels himself justified, he feels his life is in order; he boasts of this, and he judges others from his pedestal. The tax collector . . . does not multiply words. His prayer is humble, sober, pervaded by a consciousness of his own unworthiness, of his own needs. Here is a man who truly realizes that he needs God's forgiveness and mercy.

The prayer of the tax collector is the prayer of the poor man, a prayer pleasing to God. It is a prayer that, as Sirach says, "will reach to the clouds" (Sir. 35:20), unlike the prayer of the Pharisee, which is weighed down by vanity. In the light of God's word, I would like to ask you, dear families: Do you pray together from time to time as a family? Some of you do, I know. But so many people say to me, But how can we? As the tax collector does, it is clear: humbly, before God. Each one, with humility, allowing themselves to be gazed upon by the Lord and imploring his goodness, that he may visit us.

But in the family how is this done? After all, prayer seems to be something personal, and besides there is never a good time, a moment of peace. . . . Yes, all that is true enough, but it is also a matter of humility, of realizing that we need God, like the tax collector! And all families, we need God: all of us! We need his help, his strength, his blessing, his mercy, his forgiveness. And we need simplicity to pray as a family: simplicity is necessary! Praying the Our Father together, around the table, is not something extraordinary: it's easy. And praying the rosary together, as a family, is very beautiful and a source of great strength! And also praying for one another! The husband for his wife, the wife for her husband, both together for their children, the children for their grandparents. . . . praying for one another. This is what it means to pray in the family, and it is what makes the family strong: prayer.

Then, at home, your son wants to talk a little about his ideas: "Oh, I am so tired, I worked so hard today. . . ." But you sit down and listen to your son, who needs it! And you sit down, you listen to him patiently: this is a step toward sainthood. Then the day ends; we are all tired, but there are the prayers. We say our prayers: this, too, is a step toward holiness. Then comes Sunday and we go to Mass, we take communion, sometimes preceded by a beautiful confession, which cleans us a little. This is a step toward sainthood. Then we think of Our Lady, so good, so beautiful, and we take up the rosary and we pray it. This is a step toward sainthood. Then I go out to the street, I see a poor person in need, I stop and address him, I give him something: it is a step toward sainthood. These are little things, but many little steps to sanctity. Every step toward sainthood makes us better people, free from self-ishness and being closed within ourselves, and opens us to our brothers and sisters and to their needs.

Dear grandparents, dear elderly, let us follow in the footsteps of [our] extraordinary elders! Let us, too, become like poets of prayer. Let us develop a taste for finding our own words, let us once again grasp those who teach us the Word of God. *The prayer of grandparents and of the elderly is a great gift for the Church!* . . . It is a treasure! A great injection of wisdom for the whole of human society: above all for one who is too busy, too taken, too distracted. Someone should also sing . . . sing of the signs of God, proclaim the signs of God, pray for them! Let us look to Benedict XVI, who chose to spend the final span of his life in prayer and listening to God! This is beautiful! A great believer of the last century, of the Orthodox tradition, Olivier Clément, said,

"A civilization which has no place for prayer is a civilization in which old age has lost all meaning. And this is terrifying. For, above all, we need old people who pray; prayer is the purpose of old age." We need old people who pray because this is the very purpose of old age. The prayer of the elderly is a beautiful thing.

Prayer *unceasingly purifies the heart.* Praise and supplication to God prevent the heart from becoming hardened by resentment and selfishness. How awful is the cynicism of an elderly person who has lost the meaning of his testimony, who scorns the young and does not communicate the wisdom of life! How beautiful, however, is the encouragement an elderly person manages to pass on to a young person who is seeking the meaning of faith and of life! It is truly the mission of grandparents, the vocation of the elderly. The words of grandparents have special value for the young. And the young know it. I still carry with me, always, in my breviary, the words my grandmother consigned to me in writing on the day of my priestly ordination. I read them often, and they do me good.

John's Gospel states that, before his Passion, Jesus prayed to the Father for communion among his disciples, with these words: "that they may all be one; even as thou, Father, art in me, and I in thee, that they also may be in us, so that the world may believe that thou hast sent me" (John 17:21). The Church, in her most profound truth, is *communion with God*, intimacy with God, a communion of love with Christ and with the Father in the Holy Spirit, which extends to brotherly communion.

The Gospel presents Jesus in dialogue with his Father. It brings us to the heart of the prayerful intimacy between the Father and the Son. As his hour drew near, Jesus prayed for his disciples, for those with him and for those who were yet to come (John 17:20). We do well to remember that, in that crucial moment, Jesus made the lives of his disciples—our lives—a part of his prayer. He asked his Father to keep them united and joyful. Jesus knew full well the hearts of his disciples, and he knows full well our own. And so he prays to the Father to save them from a spirit of isolation, of finding refuge in their own certainties and comfort zones, of indifference to others and division into "cliques," which disfigure the richly diverse face of the Church.

It is so beautiful to know that the Lord, shortly before dying, was not concerned about himself but was thinking about us! And in his heartfelt dialogue with the Father, he prayed precisely that we might be one with him and with each other. It is with these words that Jesus made himself our intercessor with the Father, so that we, too, may enter into full communion of love with him; at the same time, he entrusts us with his spiritual testimony, so that unity may become ever more the distinctive mark of our Christian communities and the most beautiful response to whosoever asks us to account for the hope that is in us (cf. 1 Pet. 3:15).

The first reassurance we have comes from the fact that *Jesus prayed so much for the unity of the disciples.* This is the prayer of the Last Supper; Jesus asks, "Father, that they may all be one." He prayed for unity, and he actually did so as the Passion was imminent, when he was about to offer his very life for us. That is what we are continually called to reread and meditate on, in one of the most intense and moving passages in chapter 17 of the Gospel according to John (John 17:11, 21–23).

Jesus prays and he invites us to pray, because he knows that some things can be received only as gifts; some things can be experienced only as gifts. Unity is a grace that can be bestowed upon us only by the Holy Spirit; we have to ask for this grace and do our best to be transformed by that gift.

When we receive and welcome him into our heart, the Holy Spirit immediately begins to make us sensitive to his voice and to guide our thoughts, our feelings, and our intentions according to the heart of God. At the same time, he leads us more and more to turn our interior gaze to Jesus, as the model of our way of acting and of relating with God the Father and with the brethren. Counsel, then, is the gift through which the Holy Spirit *enables our conscience to make a concrete choice in communion with God,* according to the logic of Jesus and his Gospel. In this way, the Spirit makes us grow interiorly, he makes us grow positively, he makes us grow in the

> When we receive and welcome him into our heart, the Holy Spirit immediately begins to make us sensitive to his voice and to guide our thoughts, our feelings, and our intentions according to the heart of God.

community, and he helps us not to fall prey to self-centeredness and one's own way of seeing things.

The Spirit helps us to grow and also to live in community. The essential condition for preserving this gift is prayer. We always return to the same theme: prayer! Yet prayer is so important. To pray with the prayers we all learned as children, but also to pray in our own words. To ask the Lord, "Lord, help me, give me counsel, what must I do now?" And through prayer we make space so that the Spirit may come and help us in that moment, that he may counsel us on what we all must do. Prayer! Never forget prayer. Never! No one, no one realizes when we pray on the bus, on the road: we pray in the silence of our heart. Let us take advantage of these moments to pray, pray that the Spirit give us the gift of counsel. . . . It is the Spirit who counsels us, but we have to make room for the Spirit, so that he may counsel us. And to give space is to pray, to pray that he come and help us always.

There must never be a shortage of prayer, in continuity and in communion with that of Jesus, for the unity of Christians. And together with prayer, the Lord asks us for renewed openness. He asks us not to be closed to dialogue and encounter, but to welcome all that is valid and positive that is offered even by someone who thinks differently from us or who takes a different stand. He asks us not to fix our gaze on what divides us but rather on what unites us, seeking to know and love Jesus better and to share the richness of his love. And this means a concrete adherence to the Truth, together with the capacity for reciprocal forgiveness, to feel a part of the same Christian family, to consider oneself a gift for the other and together to do many good things and works of charity.

In the Gospel we hear, "Pray therefore the Lord of the harvest, to send out laborers into his harvest" (Luke 10:2). The laborers for the harvest are not chosen through advertising campaigns or appeals to service and generosity, but they are chosen and sent by God. It is he who chooses, it is he who sends; it is the Lord who sends, it is he who gives the mission. For this, prayer is important.

The Church, as Pope Benedict XVI has often reiterated, is not ours but God's; and how many times do we, consecrated men and women, think that the Church is ours! We make of it . . . something that we invent in our minds. But it is not ours! It is God's. The field to be cultivated is his. The mission is grace. And if the apostle is born of prayer, he finds in prayer the light and strength of his action. Our mission ceases to bear fruit; indeed, it is extinguished the moment the link with its source, with the Lord, is interrupted.

The passage from Revelation 12:1–6 presents the vision of the *struggle* between the woman and the dragon. The figure of the woman, representing the Church, is, on the one hand, glorious and triumphant and yet, on the other, still in travail. And the Church is like that: if in heaven she is already associated in some way with the glory of her Lord, in history she continually lives through the trials and challenges that the conflict between God and the evil one, the perennial enemy, brings. And in the struggle that the disciples must confront—all of us, all the disciples of Jesus, we must face this struggle—Mary does not leave us alone: the Mother of Christ and of the Church is always with us.

Mary walks with us always; she is with us. And in a way, Mary shares this dual condition. She has, of course, already entered, once and for all, into heavenly glory. But this does not mean that she is distant or detached from us; rather Mary accompanies us, struggles with us, sustains Christians in their fight against the forces of evil. Prayer with Mary, especially the rosary . . . has this "suffering" dimension, that is of struggle, a sustaining prayer in the battle against the evil one and his accomplices. The rosary also sustains us in the battle.

7

The Way of Human Dignity

One of the great gifts from the Second Vatican Council was that of recovering a vision of the Church founded on communion, and grasping anew the principle of authority and hierarchy in this perspective. This has helped us to better understand that all Christians, insofar as they have been baptized, are equal in dignity before the Lord and share in the same vocation—that is, to sainthood.

The Church, the "advocate of justice and defender of the poor in the face of intolerable social and economic inequalities which cry to heaven," wishes to offer her support for every initiative that can signify genuine development for every person and for the whole person. Dear friends, it is certainly necessary to give bread to the hungry—this is an act of justice. But there is also a deeper hunger, the hunger for a happiness that only God can satisfy, the hunger for dignity.

There is neither real promotion of the common good nor real human development when there is ignorance of the fundamental pillars that govern a nation, its nonmaterial goods: *life*, which is a gift of God, a value always to be protected and promoted; the *family*, the foundation of coexistence and a remedy against social fragmentation; *integral education*, which cannot be reduced to the mere transmission of information for purposes of generating profit; *health*, which must seek the integral well-being of the person, including the spiritual dimension, essential for human balance and healthy coexistence; *security*, in the conviction that violence can be overcome only by changing human hearts.

Our recent past has been marked by the concern to protect human dignity, in contrast to the manifold instances of violence and discrimination that . . . took place in the course of the centuries. Recognition of the importance of human rights came about as the result of a lengthy process, entailing much suffering and sacrifice, which helped shape an awareness of the unique worth of each individual human person. This awareness was grounded not only in historical events but above all in European thought, characterized as it is by an enriching encounter whose "distant springs are many, coming from Greece and Rome, from Celtic, Germanic and Slavic sources, and from Christianity which profoundly shaped them," thus forging the very concept of the "person."

The common home of all men and women must continue to rise on the foundations of a right understanding of universal fraternity and respect for the sacredness of every human life, of every man and every woman, the poor, the elderly, the children, the infirm, the unborn, the unemployed, the abandoned, those considered disposable because they are only considered as part of a statistic. This common home of all men and women must also be built on the understanding of a certain sacredness of created nature.

To enable real men and women to escape from extreme poverty, we must allow them to be dignified agents of their own destiny. Integral human development and the full exercise of human dignity cannot be imposed. They must be built up and allowed to unfold for each individual, for every family, in communion with others, and in a right relationship with all those areas in which human social life develops: friends, communities, towns, and cities, schools, businesses and unions, provinces, nations, etc. This presupposes and requires the right to education—also for girls (excluded in certain places)—which is ensured first and foremost by respecting and reinforcing the primary right of the family to educate its children, as well as the right of churches and social groups to support and assist families in the education of their children.

Today, the number of young people in need of work is a great burden on this global system; the unemployment rates among young people are so high. We have a generation of young people who have not yet experienced their own dignity. It isn't that they don't have anything to eat, because their grand-parents feed them, or the parish, or state-run social assistance, or the Salvation Army, or their local club. . . . They have bread to eat but not the dignity of having earned their bread to take home! Today young people have become part of this gamut of waste material.

In the throwaway culture, we find young people who need us more than ever, not only to help them with their dreams—because in a young person without work the sense of utopia is anaesthetized, or he is on the verge of losing it altogether. It is urgent to transmit the faith to young people who are looked upon today like waste material. And on the subject of waste material, drugs are spreading among these young people. It is not just a problem of vice; there are also many forms of addiction. As in all times of epic change, strange phenomena exist, such as the proliferation of dependencies: compulsive gambling has reached extremely high levels . . . and drugs are an instrument of death for young people. There is a global arming of drugs that is destroying this generation of young people, who are destined to be thrown away!

I think that this moment is the most pronounced time of anthropological reductionism. The same thing happens to man as happens when wine becomes grappa: it passes through an organizational still. It is no longer wine, it is something else: perhaps more useful, more specialized, but it's not wine! It is the same for man: man passes through this still and ends up—and I say this seriously—losing humanity and becoming an instrument of the system, the social system, economic system, a system where imbalance reigns. When man loses his humanity, what can we expect? What happens is what I would call in common parlance a policy, a sociology, a "throwaway" attitude. One discards what is not needed, because man is not at the center. And when man is not at the center, another thing is at the center, and man is at the service of this other thing.

The aim, therefore, is to save man, in the sense that he may return to the center: to the center of society, the center of thought, the center of reflection. To bring man once again to the center. . . . Children are thrown away because [of] the birth rate . . . everyone knows it; the elderly are thrown away because they are of no use. And now? A generation of young people is being thrown away, and this is most serious! I saw a figure: seventy-five million young people under twenty-five years of age without work. The young "neither-nors": neither studying nor working. They don't study because they don't have the means, and they don't work because there are no jobs. More waste. What will be the next thing thrown away? We must stop before it's too late, please!

[Along with the] lives thrown away because of war and disease, there are those [lives] of numerous refugees and displaced persons. Once again, the reality can be appreciated by reflecting on the childhood of Jesus, which sheds light on another form of the throwaway culture that harms relationships and causes the breakdown of society. Indeed, because of Herod's brutality, the Holy Family was forced to flee to Egypt and was only able to return several years later (Matt. 2:13–15). One consequence of the situations of conflict just described is the flight of thousands of persons from their homeland. At times they leave in search of not so much a better future but any future at all, since remaining at home can mean certain death. How many persons lose their lives during these cruel journeys, the victims of unscrupulous and greedy thugs? . . . Then, too, there is the alarming fact that many immigrants, especially in the Americas, are unaccompanied children, all the more at risk and in need of greater care, attention, and protection.

Our world is facing a refugee crisis of a magnitude not seen since the Second World War. This presents us with great challenges and many hard decisions. On this continent [North America], too, thousands of persons are led to travel north in search of a better life for themselves and for their loved ones, in search of greater opportunities. Is this not what we want for our own children? We must not be taken aback by their numbers but rather view them as persons, seeing their faces and listening to their stories, trying to respond as best we can to their situations. To respond in a way that is always humane, just, and fraternal. We need to avoid a common temptation nowadays: to discard whatever proves troublesome. Let us remember the Golden Rule: "Do unto others as you would have them do unto you" (Matt. 7:12).

As long as everyone seeks to accumulate for themselves, there will never be justice. We must take heed of this! As long as everyone seeks to accumulate for themselves, there will be no justice. Instead, by entrusting ourselves to God's providence and seeking his Kingdom together, no one will lack the necessary means to live with dignity.

A heart troubled by the desire for possessions is a heart full of desire for possessions but empty of God. That is why Jesus frequently warned the rich, because they greatly risk placing their security in the goods of this world, and security, the final security, is in God. In a heart possessed by wealth, there isn't much room for faith: everything is involved with wealth, there is no room for faith. If, however, one gives God his rightful place—that is, first place—then his love leads one to share even one's wealth, to set it at the service of projects of solidarity and development, as so many examples demonstrate, even recent ones, in the history of the Church. And like this, God's providence comes through our service to others, our sharing with others.

If each of us accumulates not for ourselves alone but for the service of others, in this case, in this act of solidarity, then the providence of God is made visible. If, however, one accumulates only for oneself, what will happen when one is called by God? No one can take his riches with him, because—as you know—the shroud has no pockets! It is better to share, for we can take with us to Heaven only what we have shared with others.

Peace is threatened by every denial of human dignity, firstly the lack of access to adequate nutrition. We cannot be indifferent to those suffering from hunger, especially children, when we think of how much food is wasted every day in many parts of the world immersed in what I have often termed "the throwaway culture." Unfortunately, what is thrown away is not only food and dispensable objects but often human beings themselves, who are discarded as "unnecessary." For example, it is frightful even to think that there are children, victims of abortion, who will never see the light of day; children being used as soldiers, abused and killed in armed conflicts; and children being bought and sold in that terrible form of modern slavery that is human trafficking, which is a crime against humanity.

In the end, what kind of dignity is there without the possibility of freely expressing one's thought or professing one's religious faith? What dignity can there be without a clear juridical framework that limits the rule of force and enables the rule of law to prevail over the power of tyranny? What dignity can men and women ever enjoy if they are subjected to all types of discrimination? What dignity can a person ever hope to find when he or she lacks food and the bare essentials for survival and, worse yet, when he or she lacks the work that confers dignity?

Promoting the dignity of the person means recognizing that he or she possesses inalienable rights, which no one may take away arbitrarily, much less for the sake of economic interests.

Today there is a tendency to claim ever broader individual rights [—I am tempted to say individualistic]; underlying this is a conception of the human person as detached from all social and anthropological contexts, as if the person were a "monad" (μονάς), increasingly unconcerned with other surrounding "monads." The equally essential and complementary concept of duty no longer seems to be linked to such a concept of rights. As a result, the rights of the individual are upheld without regard for the fact that each human being is part of a social context wherein his or her rights and duties are bound up with those of others and with the common good of society itself.

It is vital to develop a culture of human rights that wisely links the individual, or better, the personal aspect, to that of the *common good*, of the "*all of us*" made up of individuals, families, and intermediate groups who together constitute society. In fact, unless the rights of each individual are harmoniously ordered to the greater good, those rights will end up being considered limitless and consequently will become a source of conflicts and violence.

To speak of *transcendent human dignity* thus means appealing to human nature, to our innate capacity to distinguish good from evil, to that "compass" deep within our hearts, which God has impressed upon all creation. Above all, it means regarding human beings not as absolutes but as *beings in relation*. In my view, one of the most common diseases . . . today is the *loneliness* typical of those

> *It is vital to develop a culture of human rights that wisely links the individual, or better, the personal aspect, to that of the* common *good, of the "all of us" made up of individuals, families, and intermediate groups who together* constitute society.

who have no connection with others. This is especially true of the elderly, who are often abandoned to their fate, and also in the young who lack clear points of reference and opportunities for the future. It is also seen in the many poor who dwell in our cities and in the disorientation of immigrants who came here seeking a better future.

We encounter certain rather selfish lifestyles, marked by an opulence that is no longer sustainable and frequently indifferent to the world around us and especially to the poorest of the poor. To our dismay, we see technical and economic questions dominating political debate, to the detriment of genuine concern for human beings. Men and women risk being reduced to mere cogs in a machine that treats them as items of consumption to be exploited, with the result that—as is so tragically apparent—whenever a human life no longer proves useful for that machine, it is discarded with few qualms, as in the case of the sick, the terminally ill, the elderly who are abandoned and uncared for, and [the] children who are killed in the womb.

This is the great mistake made "when technology is allowed to take over; the result is a confusion between ends and means." It is the inevitable consequence of a throwaway culture and an uncontrolled consumerism. Upholding the dignity of the person means instead acknowledging the value of human life, which is freely given us and hence cannot be an object of trade or commerce. . . . To tend to those in need takes strength and tenderness, effort and generosity in the midst of a functionalistic and privatized mind-set that inexorably leads to a throwaway culture. To care for individuals and peoples in need means protecting memory and hope; it means taking responsibility for the present with its situations of utter marginalization and anguish and being capable of bestowing dignity upon it.

To give . . . hope means more than simply acknowledging the centrality of the human person; it also implies nurturing the gifts of each man and woman. It means investing in individuals and in those settings in which their talents are shaped and flourish. The first area surely is that of education, beginning with the family, the fundamental cell and most precious element of any society. The family united, fruitful, and indissoluble, possesses the elements fundamental for fostering hope in the future. Without this solid basis, the future ends up being built on sand, with dire social consequences. Then too, stressing the importance of the family not only helps give direction and hope to new generations but also to many of our elderly, who are often forced to live alone and are effectively abandoned because there is no longer the warmth of a family hearth able to accompany and support them.

The time has come to promote policies that create employment, but above all there is a need to restore dignity to labor by ensuring proper working conditions. This implies, on the one hand, finding new ways of joining market flexibility with the need for stability and security on the part of workers; these are indispensable for their human development. It also implies favoring a suitable social context geared not to the exploitation of persons but to ensuring, precisely through labor, their ability to create a family and educate their children.

8

The Way of the Poor

God's heart has a special place for the poor, so much so that he himself "became poor" (2 Cor. 8:9). The entire history of our redemption is marked by the presence of the poor. Salvation came to us from the "yes" uttered by a lowly maiden from a small town on the fringes of a great empire. The Savior was born . . . in the midst of animals, like children of poor families; he was presented at the Temple along with two turtledoves, the offering made by those who could not afford a lamb (Luke 2:24; Lev. 5:7); he was raised in a home of ordinary workers and worked with his own hands to earn his bread.

When he began to preach the Kingdom, crowds of the dispossessed followed him, illustrating his words: "The Spirit of the Lord is upon me, because he has anointed me to preach good news to the poor" (Luke 4:18). He assured those burdened by sorrow and crushed by poverty that God has a special place for them in his heart: "Blessed are you poor, yours is the kingdom of God" (Luke 6:20); he made himself one of them: "I was hungry and you gave me food to eat," and he taught them that mercy toward all of these is the key to heaven (cf. Matt. 25:35).

The proclamation of the Gospel is destined for the poor first of all, for all those who, all too often, lack what they need to live a dignified life. To them first are proclaimed the glad tidings that God loves them with a preferential love and comes to visit them through the charitable works that disciples of Christ do in his name. Go to the poor first of all: this is the priority. At the moment of the Last Judgment, as we can read in Matthew 25, we shall all be judged on this. Some, however, may think that Jesus' message is for those who have no cultural background. No! No! The apostle affirms forcefully that the Gospel is for everyone, even the learned. The wisdom that comes from the Resurrection is not in opposition to human wisdom but on the contrary purifies and uplifts it. The Church has always been present in places where culture is worked out. But the first step is always the priority for the poor.

The poor are at the center of the Gospel, are at the heart of the Gospel; if we take away the poor from the Gospel, we can't understand the whole message of Jesus Christ. . . . Saint Paul makes clear what this means. It means rejecting worldly perspectives and seeing all things anew in the light of Christ. It means being the first to examine our consciences, to acknowledge our failings and sins, and to embrace the path of constant conversion, everyday conversion. How can we proclaim the newness and liberating power of the Cross to others if we ourselves refuse to allow the word of God to shake our complacency, our fear of change, our petty compromises with the ways of this world, and our "spiritual worldliness"?

> *The poor are at the center of the Gospel, are at the heart of the Gospel; if we take away the poor from the Gospel, we can't understand the whole message of Jesus Christ.*

If the whole Church takes up this missionary impulse, she has to go forth to everyone without exception. But to whom should she go first? When we read the Gospel, we find a clear indication: not so much our friends and wealthy neighbors but above all the poor and the sick, those who are usually despised and overlooked, "those who cannot repay you" (Luke 14:14). There can be no room for doubt or for explanations that weaken so clear a message. Today and always "the poor are the privileged recipients of the Gospel," and the fact that it is freely preached to them is a sign of the Kingdom that Jesus came to establish. We have to state, without mincing words, that there is an inseparable bond between our faith and the poor. May we never abandon them.

The poor are also the privileged teachers of our knowledge of God; their frailty and simplicity unmask our selfishness, our false security, and our claim to be self-sufficient. The poor guide us to experience God's closeness and tenderness, to receive his love in our life, his mercy as the Father who cares for us, for all of us, with discretion and with patient trust.

The Church, which is missionary by her nature, carries out the service of charity to all as a fundamental prerogative. Universal fraternity and solidarity are connatural to her life and to her mission in the world and for the world. Evangelization, which must reach everyone, is nevertheless called to begin with the least, with the poor, with those who are weighed down by the burden and strain of life. In so doing, the Church prolongs the mission of Christ himself, who "came in order that they may have life, and have it abundantly" (John 10:10). The Church is the people of the Beatitudes, the home of the poor, of the afflicted, of the excluded and persecuted, of those who hunger and thirst for righteousness. You are asked to work and endeavor so that the ecclesial community may be ready to receive the poor with preferential love, keeping the doors of the Church open so that all may enter and find refuge therein.

The poor person, when loved, "is esteemed as of great value," and this is what makes the authentic option for the poor differ from any other ideology, from any attempt to exploit the poor for one's own personal or political interest. Only on the basis of this real and sincere closeness can we properly accompany the poor on their path of liberation. Only this will ensure that "in every Christian community the poor feel at home. Would not this approach be the greatest and most effective presentation of the good news of the kingdom?" Without the preferential option for the poor, "the proclamation of the Gospel, which is itself the prime form of charity, risks being misunderstood or submerged by the ocean of words which daily engulfs us in today's society of mass communications."

There are many poor families who try to live their daily lives with dignity, often openly entrusting themselves to God's blessing. This lesson, however, should not justify our indifference but rather increase our shame over the fact that there is so much poverty! It is almost a miracle that, even in poverty, the family continues to form and even preserve—as much as it can—the special humanity of those bonds. This fact irritates those planners of well-being who consider attachments, procreation, and familial bonds as secondary variables to the quality of life. They don't understand a thing! On the contrary, we should kneel down before these families, who are a true school of humanity in saving societies from barbarity.

We Christians have to be ever closer to the families whom poverty puts to the test. But think, all of you know someone: a father without work, a mother without work . . . and this makes the family suffer, the bonds are weakened. This is terrible. Indeed, *social destitution strikes the family and sometimes destroys it.* The lack, loss, or strong instability of employment weighs heavily upon family life, imposing a substantial strain on relationships. Living conditions in the poorest neighborhoods, with housing and transportation problems, as well as reduced social, health, and educational services, bring about further difficulties. Adding to these material factors is the damage caused to the family by the pseudo-models spread by the mass media on the basis of consumerism and the cult of appearances, which influence the poorest social classes and increase the breakdown of family ties.

Each individual Christian and every community is called to be an instrument of God for the liberation and promotion of the poor and for enabling them to be fully a part of society. This demands that we be docile and attentive to the cry of the poor and to come to their aid. A mere glance at the Scriptures is enough to make us see how our gracious Father wants to hear the cry of the poor: "I have observed the misery of my people who are in Egypt; I have heard their cry on account of their taskmasters. Indeed, I know their sufferings, and I have come down to deliver them . . . so I will send you" (Exod. 3:7–8, 10). We also see how he is concerned for their needs: "When the Israelites cried out to the Lord, the Lord raised up for them a deliverer" (Judges 3:15).

If we, who are God's means of hearing the poor, turn deaf ears to this plea, we oppose the Father's will and his plan; that poor person "might cry to the Lord against you, and you would incur guilt" (Deut. 15:9). A lack of solidarity toward his or her needs will directly affect our relationship with God: "For if in bitterness of soul he calls down a curse upon you, his Creator will hear his prayer" (Sir. 4:6). The old question always returns: "How does God's love abide in anyone who has the world's goods and sees a brother or sister in need and yet refuses help?" (1 John 3:17). Let us recall also how bluntly the apostle James speaks of the cry of the oppressed: "The wages of the laborers who mowed your fields, which you kept back by fraud, cry out, and the cries of the harvesters have reached the ears of the Lord of hosts" (James 5:4).

Jesus [invites us]: "Come to me, all who labor and are heavy laden, and I will give you rest" (Matt. 11:28). When Jesus says this, he has before him the people he meets every day on the streets of Galilee: very many simple people, the poor, the sick, sinners, those who are marginalized. . . . These people always followed him to hear his word—a word that gave hope! Jesus' words always give hope!—and even just to touch a hem of his garment. Jesus himself sought out these tired, worn-out crowds [who were] like sheep without a shepherd (Matt. 9:35–36), and he sought them out to proclaim to them the Kingdom of God and to heal many of them in body and spirit. Now he calls them all to himself: "Come to me," and he promises them relief and rest.

The Church is mother and must not forget this drama of her children. She, too, must be poor, to become fruitful and respond to so much poverty. A poor Church is a Church that practices voluntary simplicity in her life—in her very institutions, in the lifestyle of her members—to break down every dividing wall, especially to the poor. Prayer and action are needed. Let us pray earnestly that the Lord stir us, to render our Christian families leaders of this revolution of familial proximity, which is now so essential for us! The Church is made of it, of this familial proximity. Let us not forget that the judgment of the needy, of the small, and of the poor prefigures the judgment of God (Matt. 25:31–46). Let's not forget this, and let's do all we can to help families go forward in the trial of poverty and destitution that strikes attachments and family bonds.

The Gospel of Matthew presents to us the miracle of the multiplication of loaves and fish (Matt. 14:13–21). Jesus performed it along the Lake of Galilee, in a deserted place where he had withdrawn with his disciples after learning of the death of John the Baptist. But many people followed them and joined them there; and upon seeing them, Jesus felt compassion and healed their sick until the evening. And seeing the late hour, the disciples became concerned and suggested that Jesus send the crowd away so they could go into the villages and buy food to eat. But Jesus calmly replied, "You give them something to eat" (Matt. 14:16); and he asked them to bring five loaves and two fish, blessed them, began to break them and give them to the disciples, who distributed them to the people. They all ate and were satisfied, and there were even leftovers!

We can understand three messages from this event. The first is compassion. In facing the crowd who follows him and—so to speak—"won't leave him alone," Jesus does not react with irritation; he does not say, "These people are bothering me." No, no. He reacts with a feeling of compassion because he knows they are not seeking him out of curiosity but out of need. But attention: compassion—which Jesus feels—is not simply feeling pity; it's more! It means to *suffer with*, in other words, to empathize with the suffering of another to the point of taking it upon oneself.

Jesus is like this: he suffers together with us, he suffers with us, he suffers for us. And the sign of this compassion is the healing of countless people he performed. Jesus teaches us to place the needs of the poor before our own. Our needs, even if legitimate, are not as urgent as those of the poor, who lack the basic necessities of life. We often speak of the poor. But when we speak of the poor, do we sense that this man or that woman or those children lack the bare necessities of life? That they have no food, they have no clothing, they cannot afford medicine. . . . Also that the children do not have the means to attend school. Whereas our needs, although legitimate, are not as urgent as those of the poor who lack life's basic necessities.

The first [message of this event] is compassion, which Jesus felt, and the second is sharing. It's helpful to compare the reaction of the disciples in regard to the tired and hungry people, with that of Jesus. They are different. The disciples think it would be better to send them away so they can go and buy food. Jesus instead says, "You give them something to eat." Two different reactions, which reflect two contrasting outlooks: the disciples reason with worldly logic, by which each person must think of himself; they reason as if to say, "Sort it out for yourselves." Jesus reasons with God's logic, which is that of sharing.

How many times we turn away so as not to see our brothers in need! And this looking away is a polite way to say, with white gloves, "Sort it out for yourselves." And this is not Jesus' way: this is selfishness. Had he sent away the crowds, many people would have been left with nothing to eat. Instead, those few loaves and fish, shared and blessed by God, were enough for everyone. And pay heed! It isn't magic, it's a sign: a sign that calls for faith in God, provident Father, who does not let us go without "our daily bread" if we know how to share it as brothers.

The miracle of the loaves foreshadows the Eucharist. It is seen in the gesture of Jesus who, before breaking and distributing the loaves, "blessed" them (Matt. 14:19). It is the same gesture that Jesus was to make at the Last Supper when he established the perpetual memorial of his Redeeming Sacrifice. In the Eucharist Jesus does not give just any bread but *the* bread of eternal life. He gives himself, offering himself to the Father out of love for us. But we must go to the Eucharist with those sentiments of Jesus, which are compassion and the will to share. One who goes to the Eucharist without having compassion for the needy and without sharing is not at ease with Jesus.

The goodness of God has no bounds and does not discriminate against anyone. For this reason the banquet of the Lord's gifts is universal, for everyone. Everyone is given the opportunity to respond to the invitation, to his call; no one has the right to feel privileged or to claim an exclusive right. All of this induces us to break the habit of conveniently placing ourselves at the center, as did the High Priests and the Pharisees. One must not do this; we must open ourselves to the peripheries, also acknowledging that, at the margins too, even one who is cast aside and scorned by society is the object of God's generosity. We are all called not to reduce the Kingdom of God to the confines of the "little church"—our "tiny little church"—but to enlarge the Church to the dimensions of the Kingdom of God.

The Last Supper represents the culmination of Christ's entire life. It is not only the anticipation of his sacrifice, which will be rendered on the Cross, but also the synthesis of a life offered for the salvation of the whole of humanity. Therefore, it is not enough to state that Jesus is present in the Eucharist, but one must also see in it the presence of a life given and partake in it. When we take and eat that Bread, we are associated into the life of Jesus, we enter into communion with him, and we commit to achieve communion among ourselves, to transform our life into a gift, especially to the poorest.

The Christ, who nourishes us under the consecrated species of bread and wine is the same One who comes to us in the everyday happenings; he is in the poor person who holds out his hand, in the suffering one who begs for help, in the brother or sister who asks for our availability and awaits our welcome. He is in the child who knows nothing about Jesus or salvation, who does not have faith. He is in every human being, even the smallest and the [most] defenseless.

9

The Environmental Way

It must be stated that a true "right of the environment" does exist, for two reasons. First, because we human beings are part of the environment. We live in communion with it, since the environment itself entails ethical limits that human activity must acknowledge and respect. Man, for all his remarkable gifts, which "are signs of a uniqueness which transcends the spheres of physics and biology" (*Laudato Si* 81), is at the same time a part of these spheres. He possesses a body shaped by physical, chemical, and biological elements, and can survive and develop only if the ecological environment is favorable.

Any harm done to the environment, therefore, is harm done to humanity. . . . Every creature, particularly a living creature, has an intrinsic value in its existence, its life, its beauty, and its interdependence with other creatures. We Christians, together with the other monotheistic religions, believe that the universe is the fruit of a loving decision by the Creator, who permits man respectfully to use creation for the good of his fellow men and for the glory of the Creator; he is not authorized to abuse it, much less to destroy it. In all religions, the environment is a fundamental good.

[In Revelation 7:3] we heard this voice of the angel crying aloud to the four angels who were given power to damage the earth and the sea, "Do not harm earth or sea or the trees." This brought to mind a phrase that is not here but in everyone's heart: "men are far more capable of doing this better than you." We are capable of destroying the earth far better than the angels. And this is exactly what we are doing, this is what we do: destroy creation, destroy lives, destroy cultures, destroy values, destroy hope. How greatly we need the Lord's strength to seal us with his love and his power to stop this mad race of destruction! Destroying what he has given us, the most beautiful things he has done for us, so that we may carry them forward, nurture them to bear fruit.

Man takes control of everything, he believes he is God, he believes he is king. And wars, the wars that continue, they do not help to sow the seed of life but to destroy. It is an industry of destruction. It is also a system, also of life, that when things cannot be fixed, they are discarded: we discard children, we discard the old, we discard unemployed youth. This devastation has created the culture of waste.

Never more than at this moment has the world been in need of unity among people and among nations in order to overcome the divisions that exist and the current conflicts, and above all to seek concrete ways out of a crisis that is global but whose burden falls mostly on the poor. This is demonstrated precisely by food insecurity. Although it is true that it interests all countries to a varying degree, it nevertheless affects, first and foremost, the weakest part of the world's population. Let us consider the men and women, of every age and condition, who are victims of bloody conflicts and of their consequent devastation and misery, including the lack of housing, medical care, and education, and who lose every hope of a dignified life. We have an obligation toward these people, of solidarity and sharing. These obligations cannot be limited to food distribution, which can be only a "technical" remedy, more or less effective, but which terminates when what is set aside for this purpose runs out.

Sharing means to be a neighbor to all human beings, to recognize a common dignity, to understand needs and to sustain them in finding a remedy, with the same spirit of love that is lived in the family. This same love leads us to preserve creation as the most precious common good on which depends not the abstract future of the planet but the life of the human family to which it has been entrusted. This consideration calls for an education and formation capable of integrating various cultural approaches, customs, and local ways of working without substituting them in the name of an alleged cultural or technical superiority.

To defeat hunger, it is not enough to meet the needs of those who are less fortunate or to help, through aid and donations, those who live in situations of emergency. It is instead necessary to change the paradigm of aid and of development policies, to modify international laws regarding the production and trade of agricultural products, guaranteeing to countries in which agriculture represents the foundation of the economy and of survival the self-determination of their own agricultural market.

How long will we continue to defend systems of production and consumption that exclude most of the world's population even from the crumbs that fall from the tables of the rich? The time has come to think and decide, beginning with each person and community rather than from market trends. Therefore there must also be a change in the concept of work, goals, economic activity, food production, and environmental protection. This is perhaps the only possibility for building an authentic future of peace, which today is also threatened by food insecurity.

It goes without saying that part of this great effort is the creation and distribution of wealth. The right use of natural resources, the proper application of technology, and the harnessing of the spirit of enterprise are essential elements of an economy that seeks to be modern, inclusive, and sustainable. "Business is a noble vocation, directed to producing wealth and improving the world. It can be a fruitful source of prosperity for the area in which it operates, especially if it sees the creation of jobs as an essential part of its service to the common good." This common good also includes the earth, a central theme of [Laudato Si], which I recently wrote in order to "enter into dialogue with all people about our common home." "We need a conversation that includes everyone, because the environmental challenge we are undergoing, and its human roots, concern and affect us all."

Now is the time for courageous actions and strategies aimed at implementing a "culture of care" and "an integrated approach to combating poverty, restoring dignity to the excluded, and at the same time protecting nature." "We have the freedom needed to limit and direct technology"; "to devise intelligent ways of . . . developing and limiting our power"; and to put technology "at the service of another type of progress, one that is healthier, more human, more social, more integral."

[The] culture of care for the environment is not simply a "green"—I say it in the true sense of the word—attitude; it isn't just a "green" attitude, it's much more than that. Taking care of the environment means having an attitude of human ecology. That is, we cannot say that mankind is here and *creation*, the environment, is there. Ecology is total, it's human. . . . Man cannot be separated from the rest; there is a relationship that is reciprocally influential, both the environment on the person, and the person in a way that affects the environment; and the effect bounces back to man when the environment is mistreated.

[I]n society, in the social life of mankind, we cannot forget to take care of the environment. Moreover, looking after the environment is a social attitude, which socializes us, in one sense or another—each person can give it the meaning he chooses. On the other hand, it enables us to welcome—I like the Italian expression, when they speak of the environment—creation, what we are given as a gift, namely, the environment.

One of the most notable things [that happens] when the environment, when creation, isn't looked after, is the unfettered growth of cities. It is a worldwide phenomenon. It is as if the heads, the big cities, made themselves large but each time with greater areas of poverty and misery, where the people suffer the effects of environmental neglect. The phenomenon of migration is included in this sense. Why do people come to the big cities, to the poverty belts of big cities: the shanty towns, slums, and favelas? Why do they do this? It is simply because the rural world doesn't offer them opportunities.

[The idolatry of] technocracy leads to the destruction of jobs; it creates unemployment. The phenomena of *unemployment* are widespread, and people are forced to emigrate, seeking new horizons. The high number of unemployed people is alarming. . . . Projecting into the future, this makes us see a ghost, in other words, an unemployed body of youth, which today is offered what horizon and what future? What is left for these young people: addiction, boredom, not knowing what to do with one's life—a very hard life without meaning. [What is left:] youth suicide—the statistics on suicide among young people have not been published in their entirety—or searching for an ideal life under other horizons, even in guerrilla projects.

What happens when all these phenomena of excessive technicization, without caring for the environment, in addition to natural phenomena, affect migration? Unemployment and then human trafficking. Illegal work, without contracts; working "under the table" is occurring more and more frequently. How it has increased! Illegal work is truly pervasive, and this means that people don't earn enough to live. This can lead to criminal behavior [and] all the problems that occur in large cities due to these migrations caused by excessive technicization.

I refer in particular to the agricultural environment and also to human trafficking in the mining industry. Slavery in mines is a major issue. It involves the use of certain elements in the treatment of minerals—arsenic and cyanide, which cause diseases in the population. There is a very great responsibility in this. It all bounces back, it all turns around; everything has a rebound affect against the person himself. It can include human trafficking for purposes of slave labor or prostitution, sources of work to enable survival today.

[Romano Guardini] speaks of two forms of ignorance: the ignorance that God gave us, to be transformed into culture, which is why he gave us the mandate to care for, make fruitful and have dominion over the earth; the second form of ignorance, when man fails to respect this relationship with the earth and doesn't look after it—it's very clear in the biblical account, it's a mystical sort of reading. When he does not look after it, man falls prey to this second form of ignorance and steers the earth off its intended course. It is ignorance—that is to say, man changing its course, losing control of it, thus giving rise to a second form of ignorance.

Atomic energy is good; it can be helpful. Up to a point it's okay, but let's think about Hiroshima and Nagasaki. In other words, [atomic energy can create disaster and destruction]. . . . In a midrash, a medieval rabbi from about the time of St. Thomas Aquinas . . . explained the problem of the Tower of Babel to his "parishioners" in the synagogue. He said that building the Tower of Babel took a lot of time and work, especially in making the bricks. It called for preparing mud, finding hay, baling it, cutting it, drying it, then putting it in the oven, baking. . . . Each brick was like a gem; they were really valuable. They carried the bricks up to place them on the tower. When a brick fell it was a very serious problem, and the culprit who had neglected his work and dropped the brick was punished. When a construction worker fell, nothing would happen. This is the tragedy of the second form of ignorance: man as creator of ignorance rather than culture; man as creator of ignorance because he doesn't care for the environment.

The vocation of being a "protector," however, is not just something involving us Christians alone; it also has a prior dimension that is simply human, involving everyone. It means protecting all creation, the beauty of the created world, as the book of Genesis tells us and as Saint Francis of Assisi showed us. It means respecting each of God's creatures and respecting the environment in which we live. It means protecting people, showing loving concern for each and every person, especially children, the elderly, those in need, who are often the last we think about. It means caring for one another in our families: husbands and wives first protect one another, and then, as parents, they care for their children, and children themselves, in time, protect their parents. It means building sincere friendships in which we protect one another in trust, respect, and goodness. In the end, everything has been entrusted to our protection, and all of us are responsible for it. Be protectors of God's gifts!

Please, I would like to ask all those who have positions of responsibility in economic, political, and social life, and all men and women of goodwill: let us be protectors of creation, protectors of God's plan inscribed in nature, protectors of one another and of the environment. Let us not allow omens of destruction and death to accompany the advance of this world! But to be protectors we also have to keep watch over ourselves! Let us not forget that hatred, envy, and pride defile our lives! Being protectors, then, also means keeping watch over our emotions, over our hearts, because they are the seat of good and evil intentions, intentions that build up and tear down! We must not be afraid of goodness or even tenderness!

Our earth needs constant concern and attention. Each of us has a personal responsibility to
care for creation, this precious gift God has
entrusted to us. This means, on the one hand,
that nature is at our disposal, to enjoy and use
properly. Yet it also means that we are not its
masters. Stewards, but not masters. We need to
love and respect nature, but "instead we are
often guided by the pride of dominating, possessing, manipulating, exploit-
ing; we do not 'preserve' the earth, we do not respect it, we do not consider it
as a freely-given gift to look after."

Our earth needs constant concern and attention. Each of us has a personal responsibility to care for creation, this precious gift God has entrusted to us.

Respect for the environment, however, means more than not destroying it;
it also means using it for good purposes. I am thinking above all of the agricultural sector, which provides sustenance and nourishment to our human
family. It is intolerable that millions of people around the world are dying of
hunger while tons of food are discarded each day from our tables. Respect
for nature also calls for recognizing that man himself is a fundamental part
of it. Along with an environmental ecology, there is also need of that human
ecology that consists of respect for the person.

Our attitude . . . is the attitude of the Beatitudes. That path alone will lead
us to the encounter with God. That path alone will save us from destruction, from destroying the earth—creation, morality, history, family, everything. That path alone. But it, too, will bring us through bad things! It will
bring us problems and persecution. But that path alone will take us forward.
And so, these people who are suffering so much today because of the selfishness of destroyers, of our brothers' destroyers, these people struggle onward
with the Beatitudes, with the hope of finding God, of coming face-to-face
with the Lord in the hope of becoming saints at the moment of our final
encounter with him.

10

The Way of Families

The family is in crisis: this is true and it's not news. Young people don't want to get married; they would rather relax, live together with no commitment. Then, if they have a child, they will be forced to get married. Nowadays getting married isn't in fashion! How many times I have asked at a wedding in a church, "You, who are here to get married, are you doing so because you want to enter the Sacrament with your fiancée or because this is just what people do in society?" A short time ago a couple, after living together for a long time, decided to get married. "When?" "We still don't know; we are looking for a church that goes with the dress, and then we are looking for a restaurant that is near the church, and then we need to pick the party favors, and then. . . ." "But tell me: with what faith are you getting married?"

Preparing for marriage is not like taking a class, like a language course: becoming husband and wife in eight classes. Preparing for marriage is something else. It must begin at home, with friends, from youth, from engagement. The period of engagement has lost its sacred sense of respect. Today, being engaged and living together are practically the same thing. Not always, because there are some beautiful examples. . . . How can we help an engagement mature? For when an engagement is healthy, the time comes when you ought to marry, because the engagement is mature. It is like fruit: if you don't harvest it while it's ripe, it will no longer be good. Everything is in crisis, and I ask you to pray a lot. I do not have the recipe for this. But the testimony of love, the testimony of how to solve problems is important.

Let us think about our parents, about our grandparents and great-grandparents: they married in much poorer conditions than our own. Some married during wartime or just after a war. Some, like my own parents, emigrated. Where did they find the strength? They found it in the certainty that the Lord was with them, that their families were blessed by God through the sacrament of matrimony, and that the mission of bringing children into the world and educating them was also blessed. With this assurance they overcame even the most difficult trials. These were simple certainties, but they were real; they were the pillars that supported their love. Their lives were not easy; there were problems, many, many problems. However, these simple assurances helped them go forward. And they succeeded in having beautiful families and in giving life and in raising their children.

Yes, it is so true that it takes courage to form a family. It takes courage! And your question, young spouses, is linked to *the question of vocation*. What is marriage? It is *a true and authentic vocation*, as are the priesthood and the religious life. Two Christians who marry have recognized the call of the Lord in their own love story, the vocation to form one flesh and one life from two, male and female. And the sacrament of holy matrimony envelops this love in the grace of God—it roots it in God himself. By this gift, and by the certainty of this call, you can continue on assured; you have nothing to fear; you can face everything together!

With trust in God's faithfulness, everything can be faced responsibly and without fear. Christian spouses are not naive; they know life's problems and temptations. But they are not afraid to be responsible before God and before society. They do not run away, they do not hide, they do not shirk the mission of forming a family and bringing children into the world. "But today, Father, it is difficult. . . ." Of course it is difficult! That is why we need the grace, the grace that comes from the sacrament! The sacraments are not decorations in life—what a beautiful marriage, what a beautiful ceremony, what a beautiful banquet. . . . But that is not the sacrament of marriage. That is a decoration! Grace is not given to decorate life but rather to make us strong in life, giving us courage to go forward! And without isolating oneself but always staying together. Christians celebrate the sacrament of marriage because they know they need it! They need it to stay together and to carry out their mission as parents.

"In joy and in sadness, in sickness and in health." This is what the spouses say to each other during the celebration of the sacrament, and in their marriage they pray with one another and with the community. Why? Because it is helpful to do so? No! They do so because they need to, for the long journey they are making together: it is a long journey, not for a brief spell but for an entire life! And they need Jesus' help to walk beside one another in trust, to accept one another each day, and daily to forgive each other. And this is important! To know how to forgive one another in families because we all make mistakes, all of us! Sometimes we do things that are not good and that harm others. It is important to have the courage to ask for forgiveness when we are at fault in the family.

In order to have a healthy family, three phrases need to be used. And I want to repeat these three phrases: please, thank you, sorry. Three essential phrases! We say please so as not to be forceful in family life: "May I please do this? Would you be happy if I did this?" We do this with a language that seeks agreement. We say thank you, thank you for love! But be honest with me, how many times do you say thank you to your wife, to your husband? How many days go by without uttering this word, thanks? And the last word: sorry. We all make mistakes, and on occasion someone gets offended in the marriage, in the family, and sometimes . . . plates are smashed, harsh words are spoken, but please listen to my advice: don't ever let the sun set without reconciling. Peace is made each day in the family: "Please forgive me" and then you start over. . . . Let us say these words in our families. To forgive one another each day!

In marriage there is also fighting. . . . I try to give practical advice: fight as much as you want, but don't end the day without making peace. In order to do this, you don't have to get on your knees; a caress would suffice. Because whenever you fight, you build up resentment inside, and if you make peace immediately, it's ok. However, the cold resentment of the day before is much harder to move past. Therefore make peace that same day.

It is always important to ask the other if he or she likes something. You are together, in a marriage; "I" is not good, "we" is much more effective. What they say about marriage is also true: joy for two—three times more joy; pain and suffering—half the pain and half the suffering. Married life should be lived like this, and this is done through prayer, a great deal of prayer and witness so that the love doesn't burn out. Because there will always be difficult trials in life, and we cannot cherish the illusion of finding another person and saying, "Oh, had I only met this person before, I would have married him or her." Well, you didn't meet him before, he came too late. Close the door now! Be attentive to these things and move forward with your testimony. And thus I am back where I started: the family is in crisis and it is not easy to answer; however, testimony and prayer are necessary.

Dear parents, your children need to discover, to see in your life, the beauty of loving one another. Don't ever forget that your children are always watching you. . . . Children watch. They watch closely, and when they see that Daddy and Mommy love each other, the children grow up in that atmosphere of love and happiness as well as security because they are not afraid: they know they are safe in the love of their father and mother.

There is no greater testimony for a child than seeing his own parents love one another tenderly, respect one another, be kind to each other, forgive one another; this fills children's hearts with true joy and happiness. Before dwelling in a house made of bricks, children dwell in another house, which is even more essential: they dwell in the reciprocal love of their parents. I ask you, every one, to answer in your heart: do your children abide in your mutual love? Parents have the vocation to love one another. God has sowed in their hearts the vocation to love because God is love. And this is your vocation as parents: love. However, always think of the children, always think of the children!

> *There is no greater testimony for a child than seeing his own parents love one another tenderly, respect one another, be kind to each other, forgive one another.*

You are collaborators with the Holy Spirit, who whispers Jesus' words to you! Be the same for your children! Be missionaries to your children. They will learn from your lips and from your life that following the Lord gives one enthusiasm, a desire to spend oneself for others; it always gives hope, even in the face of difficulties and sorrow, because we are never alone but always with the Lord and with our brothers and sisters. And this is important especially in preadolescence, when the search for God becomes more conscious and the questions call for well-founded answers.

Let us think how much children suffer when they see their father and mother shout at one another, insult one another, even hit one another on a daily basis. But, Dad and Mom, when you fall into these sins, do you realize that the first victims are in fact your children, your very own flesh and blood? It's an awful thing to think of, but it is a reality. . . . Children watch us. They don't look at you only when you are teaching them something. They look at you when you speak to each other, when you come home from work, when you invite your friends over, when you are resting. They try to grasp from your eyes, from your words, from your gestures, if you are happy being parents, if you are happy being husband and wife, if you believe that goodness exists in the world. They scrutinize you—they don't just watch you, they scrutinize you—to see if it's possible to be good and if it's true that with mutual love every difficulty is surmounted.

[Some children are] orphans, without the memory of their families: because, for example, grandparents are far away or in a retirement home, they don't have that familial presence, that familial memory. [Other children are] without affection today, or with a kind of affection that is frantic: Dad is tired, Mom is tired, they go to bed. . . . And [the children] are left orphans. [Such children also miss] the generosity of a dad and a mom who know how to waste time just playing with their children. We need that sense of gratuitousness: in families, in parishes, and in society as a whole. And when we think of how the Lord is revealed to us through the free gift, that is, grace, it's a much more important thing. That need for human gratuitousness, which is how we open our hearts to the grace of God. Everything is free: he comes and grants us his grace. But if we don't have a sense of gratuitousness in the family, at school, in the parish, it will be very difficult for us to understand what the grace of God is, the grace that isn't sold, that isn't bought, but a present, a gift from God: it is God himself.

Are grandparents given a place of dignity in the family? Now I'm sure that they are, because with all the unemployment, people go to their grandparents for their pension. Yes, this happens. But do grandparents, who are the wisdom of a people, the memory of a people, the wisdom of the family, have a place of honor? It has been the grandparents who saved the faith in so many countries where it was prohibited to practice religion, taking the children secretly to have them baptized, and it has been the grandparents who taught them prayers.

I'm sure I've already told this story, a story I heard as a child, in my home. It was said that in one family the grandfather lived with his son, his daughter-in-law, and his grandchildren. But the grandfather had grown old, he had had a stroke . . . he was old and when he sat at the table to eat, he would spill a little [food on] himself. The dad was ashamed of his own father and said, "We can't invite people to our home." So he decided to make a small table in the kitchen for the grandfather to eat at alone. This is how it went. A few days later, he came home from work and found his son—six or seven years old—who was playing with wood, a hammer, and nails. "What are you doing, boy?" "I am making a small table." "Why?" "So that when you are old you will be able to eat alone like Grandpa!" Don't be ashamed of the grandfather. Don't be ashamed of the elderly. They give us wisdom, prudence, they help us so much. When they get sick, they require so many sacrifices from us, it's true. Sometimes there is no solution other than taking them to a nursing home. But let it be the last, the last resort. Grandparents in the home are a wealth.

We live nowadays in immense cities that show off proudly, even arrogantly, how modern they are. But while they offer well-being and innumerable pleasures for a happy minority, housing is denied to thousands of our neighbors, our brothers and sisters including children, who are called elegant names such as "street people" or those "without fixed abode" or "urban campers." Isn't it curious how euphemisms abound in the world of injustices! A person, a segregated person, a person set apart, a person who suffers misery or hunger: such a one is an "urban camper."

I said it, and I repeat it: a home for every family. We must never forget that, because there was no room in the inn, Jesus was born in a stable. His family, persecuted by Herod, had to leave their home and flee into Egypt. Today there are so many homeless families, either because they have never had a home or because, for different reasons, they have lost it. Family and housing go hand in hand. Furthermore, for a house to be a home, it requires a community dimension, and this is the neighborhood . . . and it is precisely in the neighborhood where the great family of humanity begins to be built, starting from the most immediate instance, from living together with one's neighbors.

Let yourselves be healed by Jesus. We all have wounds, everyone: spiritual wounds, sins, hostility, jealousy; perhaps we don't say hello to someone: "Ah, he did this to me, I won't acknowledge him anymore." But this needs to be healed! "How do I do it?" Pray and ask that Jesus heal it. It's sad in a family when siblings don't speak to each other over a small matter, because the devil takes a small matter and makes a world of it. Then hostilities go on, oftentimes for many years, and that family is destroyed. Parents suffer because their children don't speak to each other, or one son's wife doesn't speak to the other, and thus, with jealousy, envy. . . . The devil sows this. And the only One who casts out demons is Jesus. The only One who heals these matters is Jesus.

For this reason I say to each one of you: let yourself be healed by Jesus. Each one knows where his wounds are. Each one of us has them; we don't have only one: two, three, four, twenty. Each one knows! May Jesus heal those wounds. But for this I must open my heart, in order that he may come. How do I open my heart? By praying. "But, Lord, I can't with those people over there. I hate them. They did this, this, and this . . ." "Heal this wound, Lord." If we ask Jesus for this grace, he will do it. Let yourself be healed by Jesus. Let Jesus heal you. Let Jesus preach to you and let him heal you. This way I can even preach to others, to teach the words of Jesus, because I let him preach to me. And I can also help heal many wounds, the many wounds that there are. But first I have to do it: let him preach to me and heal me.

11

The Way of Children

I would like to talk about the child, or even better, about children. I shall use a beautiful image from Isaiah. The prophet writes, "They all gather together, they come to you; your sons shall come from far, and your daughters shall be carried in the arms. Then you shall see and be radiant, your heart shall thrill and rejoice" (Isa. 60:4–5). It is a splendid image, an image of happiness that is fulfilled in the reunion of parents and children who journey together toward a future of freedom and peace after a long period of deprivation and separation, when the Hebrew people were far from their homeland.

We must consider this carefully. There is a close link between the hope of a people and the harmony among generations. The joy of children causes the parents' hearts to beat and reopens the future. Children are the joy of the family and of society. They are not a question of reproductive biology or one of the many ways to fulfill oneself, much less a possession of their parents. . . . No. Children are a gift, they are a gift—understood? Children are a gift. Each one is unique and irreplaceable and at the same time unmistakably linked to his or her roots.

First of all children remind us that we all, in the first years of life, were completely dependent upon the care and benevolence of others. The Son of God was not spared this stage. It is the mystery that we contemplate every year at Christmas. The nativity scene is the icon that communicates this reality in the simplest and most direct way. It is curious: God has no difficulty in making himself understood by children, and children have no difficulty in understanding God.

It is not by chance that in the Gospel there are several very beautiful and powerful words of Jesus regarding the "little ones." This term, *babes*, refers to all the people who depend on the help of others, and to children in particular. For example, Jesus says, "I thank thee, Father, Lord of heaven and earth, that thou hast hidden these things from the wise and understanding, and revealed them to babes" (Matt. 11:25). And again: "See that you do not despise one of these little ones: for I tell you that in heaven their angels always behold the face of my Father who is in heaven" (Matt. 18:10).

Once Jesus rebuked his disciples because they sent away the children whose parents brought them to him to be blessed. It is a moving Gospel narrative: "Then children were brought to him that he might lay his hands on them and pray. The disciples rebuked the people, but Jesus said, 'Let the children come to me, and do not hinder them; for to such belongs the kingdom of heaven.' And he laid his hands on them and went away" (Matt. 19:13–15). How beautiful is the parents' trust and Jesus' response! How I would like this passage to become the norm for all children! It is true that by the grace of God children in grave difficulty are often given extraordinary parents, ready and willing to make every sacrifice. But these parents should not be left alone! We should accompany them in their toil and also offer them moments of shared joy and lighthearted cheer, so that they are not left with only routine therapy.

[Mark chapter five] presents the account of the resurrection of a young twelve-year-old girl, the daughter of one of the leaders of the synagogue, who falls at Jesus' feet and beseeches him: "My little daughter is at the point of death. Come and lay your hands on her, so that she may be made well, and live." In this prayer we hear the concern of every father for the life and well-being of his child. We also hear the great faith that this man has in Jesus. And when news arrives that the little girl is dead, Jesus tells him, "Do not fear, only believe" (Mark 5:36). These words from Jesus give us courage! And he frequently also says to us, "Do not fear, only believe." Entering the house, the Lord sends away all those who are weeping and wailing and turns to the dead girl, saying, "Little girl, I say to you, arise" (Mark 5:41). And immediately the little girl rises and begins to walk. Here we see Jesus' absolute power over death, which for him is like a dream from which one can awaken.

Children are in and of themselves a treasure for humanity and also for the Church, for they constantly evoke that necessary condition for entering the Kingdom of God: that of not considering ourselves self-sufficient but in need of help, love, and forgiveness. We all are in need of help, love, and forgiveness! Children remind us of another beautiful thing: . . . we are always sons and daughters. Even if one becomes an adult, or an elder, even if one becomes a parent, if one occupies a position of responsibility—underneath all of this is still the identity of a child.

We are all sons and daughters. And this always brings us back to the fact that we did not give ourselves life but that we received it. The great gift of life is the first gift we received. Sometimes we risk forgetting about this, as if we were the masters of our existence, but instead we are fundamentally dependent. In reality, it is a motive of great joy to feel at every stage of life, in every situation, in every social condition, that we are and we remain sons and daughters. This is the main message children give us by their very presence; simply by their presence they remind us that each and every one of us is a son or daughter.

A child has spontaneous trust in his father and mother; he has spontaneous trust in God, in Jesus, in Our Lady. At the same time, his interior gaze is pure, not yet tainted by malice, by duplicity, by the "incrustations" of life that harden the heart. We know that children are also marked by original sin, that they are selfish, but they preserve purity and interior simplicity. But children are not diplomats: they say what they feel, say what they see, directly. And so often they put their parents in difficulty, saying in front of other people, "I don't like this because it is ugly." But children say what they see; they are not two-faced, they have not yet learned that science of duplicity that we adults have unfortunately learned. . . . Children—in their interior simplicity—bring with them the capacity to receive and give tenderness. Tenderness is having a heart "of flesh" and not "of stone," as the Bible says (cf. Ezek. 36:26). Tenderness is also poetry: it is feeling things and events, not treating them as mere objects, only to use them, because they are useful.

Children have the capacity to smile and to cry. Some, when I pick them up to embrace them, smile. Others see me dressed in white and think I am a doctor and that I am going to vaccinate them, and they cry . . . spontaneously! Children are like this: they smile and cry, two things that are often stifled in grown-ups. We are no longer capable. . . . So often our smile becomes a cardboard smile, fixed, a smile that is not natural, even an artificial smile, like a clown's. Children smile spontaneously and cry spontaneously. It always depends on the heart, and often our heart is blocked and loses this capacity to smile, to cry. So children can teach us how to smile and cry again. But we must ask ourselves, do I smile spontaneously, frankly, with love, or is my smile artificial? Do I still cry, or have I lost the capacity to cry? These are two very human questions that children teach us. . . . For all these reasons Jesus invited his disciples to "become like children" because "the Kingdom of God belongs to those who are like them" (Matt. 18:3; Mark 10:14).

Despite our seemingly evolved sensitivity and all our refined psychological analyses, I ask myself if we are not just anesthetizing ourselves to the wounds in children's souls. The more you try to compensate with gifts and snacks, the more you lose your sense of these spiritual wounds—so painful and so deep. We talk a lot about behavioral problems, mental health, the well-being of the child, about the anxiety of parents and their children. . . . But do we even know what a spiritual wound is? Do we feel the weight of the mountain that crushes the soul of a child in those families where members mistreat and hurt one another to the point of breaking the bonds of marital fidelity? How much weight do our choices have—mistaken choices, for example—how much weight do they place on the soul of our children? When adults lose their heads, when each one thinks only of him- or herself, when a dad and mom hurt each other, the souls of their children suffer terribly, they experience a sense of despair. And these wounds leave a mark that lasts their whole lives.

The weakness and suffering of our dearest and most cherished loved ones can be, for our children and grandchildren, a school of life—it's important to teach the children and grandchildren to understand this closeness during illness at home—and they become [close] when times of illness are accompanied by prayer and the affectionate and thoughtful closeness of relatives. The Christian community really knows that the family, in the trial of illness, should not be left on its own. We must say thank you to the Lord for those beautiful experiences of ecclesial fraternity that help families get through the difficult moments of pain and suffering. This Christian closeness, from family to family, is a real treasure for the parish; it's a treasure of wisdom, which helps families in the difficult moments to understand the Kingdom of God better than many discourses! They are God's caresses.

From the first moments of their lives, many children are rejected, abandoned, and robbed of their childhood and future. There are those who dare to say, as if to justify themselves, that it was a mistake to bring these children into the world. This is shameful! Let's not unload our faults onto the children, please! Children are never a mistake. Their hunger is not a mistake, nor is their poverty, their vulnerability, their abandonment—so many children abandoned on the streets—and neither is their ignorance or their helplessness. . . . So many children don't even know what a school is. If anything, these should be reasons to love them all the more, with greater generosity. How can we make such solemn declarations on human rights and the rights of children, if we then punish children for the errors of adults?

Every child who is marginalized, abandoned, who lives on the street begging with every kind of trick, without schooling, without medical care, is a cry that rises up to God and denounces the system that we adults have set in place. And unfortunately these children are prey to criminals who exploit them for shameful trafficking or commerce, or who train them for war and violence. But even in so-called wealthy countries many children live in dramatic situations that scar them deeply because of crises in the family, educational gaps, and at times inhuman living conditions. In every case, their childhood is violated in body and soul. But none of these children is forgotten by the Father who is in

> *Every child who is marginalized, abandoned, without schooling, without medical care, is a cry that rises up to God and denounces the system that we adults have set in place.*

heaven! Not one of their tears is lost! Neither is our responsibility lost, the social responsibility of people, of each one of us, and of countries.

A mother then thinks of the health of her children, teaching them also *to face the difficulties of life*. You do not teach, you do not take care of health by avoiding problems, as though life were a motorway with no obstacles. The mother helps her children see the problems of life realistically and [teaches] not to get lost in them but to confront them with courage, not to be weak but to know how to overcome them, in a healthy balance that a mother senses between the area of security and the area of risk. And a mother can do this! She does not always take the child along the safe road, because in that way the child cannot develop, but neither does she leave the child only on the risky path, because that is dangerous. A mother knows how to balance things. A life without challenges does not exist, and a boy or a girl who cannot face or tackle them is a boy or girl with no backbone.

A child is loved because he is one's child, not because he is beautiful, or because he is like this or like that—no, because he is a child! Not because he thinks as I do or embodies my dreams. A child is a child: a life generated by us but intended for him, for his good, for the good of the family, of society, of mankind as a whole.

Think what a society would be like if it decided, once and for all, to establish this principle: "It's true, we are not perfect, and we make many mistakes. But when it comes to the children who come into the world, no sacrifice on the part of adults is too costly or too great to ensure that no child believes he or she was a mistake, is worthless, or is abandoned to a life of wounds and to the arrogance of men." How beautiful a society like this would be! I say that for such a society, much could be forgiven, innumerable errors. Truly a great deal.

[There is] depth in the human experience of being a son or daughter, which allows us to discover the most gratuitous dimension of love, which never ceases to astonish us. It is the beauty of being loved first: children are loved before they arrive. So often I find mothers in the square who are expecting a baby and ask me for a blessing . . . these babies are loved before coming into the world. And this is free, this is love; they are loved before being born, like the love of God who always loves us first. They are loved before having done anything to deserve it, before knowing how to talk or think, even before coming into the world! Being children is the basic condition for knowing the love of God, which is the ultimate source of this authentic miracle. In the soul of every child, inasmuch as it is vulnerable, God places the seal of this love, which is at the basis of his or her personal dignity, a dignity that nothing and no one can ever destroy.

In a frail human being, each one of us is invited to recognize the face of the Lord, who in his human flesh experienced the indifference and solitude to which we so often condemn the poorest of the poor, whether in developing countries or in wealthy societies. Every child who, rather than being born, is condemned unjustly to being aborted, bears the face of Jesus Christ, bears the face of the Lord, who even before he was born, and then just after birth, experienced the world's rejection. And every elderly person—I spoke of children: let us move to the elderly, another point! And every elderly person, even if he is ill or at the end of his days, bears the face of Christ. They cannot be discarded, as the culture of waste suggests! They cannot be thrown away!

The fourth commandment asks children—we are all children!—to honor our father and mother (cf. Exod. 20:12). This commandment comes immediately after those regarding God himself. Indeed, it contains something sacred, something divine, something that lies at the root of every other type of respect among men. And to the biblical formulation of the fourth commandment is added, "that your days may be long in the land which the Lord your God gives you." The virtuous bond between generations is the guarantee of the future and is the guarantee of a truly human history. A society with children who do not honor parents is a society without honor; when one does not honor one's parents, one loses one's own honor! It is a society destined to be filled with arid and avid young people.

May the Lord bless our parents and bless your children. May Jesus, the eternal Son who in the fullness of time became a child, help us find the path of a new radiation of this so great and so simple human experience of being children. In the multiplication of generations there is a mystery of enrichment of the life of all, which comes from God himself. We must rediscover it, challenging prejudice, and live it, in the faith, in perfect happiness. And I say to you: how beautiful it is when I pass in your midst and I see the dads and moms lift up their children to be blessed; this is an almost divine gesture.

12

Mary: Mother and Companion on the Way

How was Mary's faith a journey? In the sense that her entire life was to follow her Son: he—Jesus—is the way, he is the path! To press forward in faith, to advance in the spiritual pilgrimage that is faith, is nothing other than to follow Jesus: to listen to him and be guided by his words; to see how he acts and follow in his footsteps; to have his same sentiments. And what are these sentiments of Jesus? Humility, mercy, closeness to others, but also a firm rejection of hypocrisy, duplicity, and idolatry. The way of Jesus is the way of a love that is faithful to the end, even unto sacrificing one's life; it is the way of the Cross. The journey of faith thus passes through the Cross. Mary understood this from the beginning, when Herod sought to kill the newborn Jesus. But then this experience of the Cross became deeper when Jesus was rejected.

Mary was always with Jesus; she followed him in the midst of the crowds, and she heard all the gossip and the nastiness of those who opposed the Lord. And she carried this cross! Mary's faith encountered misunderstanding and contempt. When Jesus' "hour" came, the hour of his passion, Mary's faith was a little flame burning in the night, a little light flickering in the darkness. Through the night of Holy Saturday, Mary kept watch. Her flame, small but bright, remained burning until the dawn of the Resurrection. And when she received word that the tomb was empty, her heart was filled with the joy of faith: Christian faith in the death and resurrection of Jesus Christ.

Our pilgrimage of faith has been inseparably linked to Mary ever since Jesus, dying on the Cross, gave her to us as our Mother, saying, "Behold your Mother!" (John 19:27). These words serve as a testament, bequeathing to the world a Mother. From that moment on, the Mother of God also became our Mother! When the faith of the disciples was most tested by difficulties and uncertainties, Jesus entrusted them to Mary, who was the first to believe, and whose faith would never fail.

The "woman" became our Mother when she lost her divine Son. Her sorrowing heart was enlarged to make room for all men and women—all, whether good or bad—and she loves them as she loved Jesus. The woman who at the wedding at Cana in Galilee gave her faith-filled cooperation so that the wonders of God could be displayed in the world, at Calvary kept alive the flame of faith in the resurrection of her Son, and she communicates this with maternal affection to each and every person. Mary becomes in this way a source of hope and true joy!

> *Mary became our Mother when she lost her divine Son. Her sorrowing heart was enlarged to make room for all men and women—all, whether good or bad—and she loves them as she loved Jesus.*

In celebrating [the Assumption], we join the Church throughout the world in looking to Mary as our Mother of Hope. Her song of praise reminds us that God never forgets his promise of mercy (Luke 1:54–55). Mary is the one who is blessed because "she believed that there would be a fulfillment of what was spoken to her by the Lord" (Luke 1:45). In her, all God's promises have been proved trustworthy. Enthroned in glory, she shows us that our hope is real; even now it reaches as "a sure and steadfast anchor of the soul" (Heb. 6:19) to where Jesus is seated in glory.

We can imagine that the Virgin Mary, visiting the home of Elizabeth, would have heard her and her husband, Zechariah, praying in the words of today's responsorial psalm: "You, O Lord, are my hope, my trust, O Lord, from my youth. . . . Do not cast me off in the time of old age, do not forsake me when my strength is spent. . . . Even to old age and grey hairs, O God, do not forsake me, until I proclaim your might to all the generations to come" (Ps. 71:5, 9, 18). The young Mary listened, and she kept all these things in her heart. The wisdom of Elizabeth and Zechariah enriched her young spirit. They were no experts in parenthood; for them, too, it was the first pregnancy.

But they were experts in faith, experts in God, experts in the hope that comes from him. And this is what the world needs in every age. Mary was able to listen to those elderly and amazed parents; she treasured their wisdom, and it proved precious for her in her journey as a woman, as a wife, and as a mother.

Mary is not in a hurry, she does not let herself be swept away by the moment; she does not let herself be dragged along by events. However, when she has clearly understood what God is asking of her, what she has to do, she does not loiter; she does not delay but goes "with haste." St. Ambrose commented, "There is nothing slow about the Holy Spirit." Mary's action was a consequence of her obedience to the angel's words but was combined with charity: she went to Elizabeth to make herself useful; and in going out of her home, of herself, for love, she takes with her the most precious thing she has: Jesus. She takes her Son.

What gave rise to Mary's act of going to visit her relative Elizabeth? A word of God's angel. "Elizabeth in her old age has also conceived a son . . ." (Luke 1:36). Mary knew how to listen to God. . . . [I]t was not merely hearing, [which can be] superficial . . . but it was listening, which consists of attention, acceptance, and availability to God. It was not in the distracted way with which we sometimes face the Lord or others: we hear their words, but we do not really listen. Mary is attentive to God. She listens to God. However, Mary also listens to the events—that is, she interprets the events of her life. She is attentive to reality itself and does not stop on the surface but goes to the depths to grasp its meaning. Her kinswoman Elizabeth, who is already elderly, is expecting a child: this is the event. But Mary is attentive to the meaning. She can understand it: "With God nothing will be impossible" (Luke 1:37).

We heard the Song of Mary, the *Magnificat* [Luke 1:46–55]: it is the song of hope, it is the song of the People of God walking through history. It is the song [of] many saints, men and women, some famous, and very many others unknown to us but known to God: moms, dads, catechists, missionaries, priests, sisters, young people, even children and grandparents. These have faced the struggle of life while carrying in their hearts the hope of the little and the humble. Mary says, "My soul glorifies the Lord." Today, the Church, too, sings this in every part of the world. This song is particularly strong in places where the Body of Christ is suffering the Passion.

For us Christians, wherever the Cross is, there is hope, always. If there is no hope, we are not Christian. That is why I like to say: do not allow yourselves to be robbed of hope. May we not be robbed of hope, because this strength is a grace, a gift from God that carries us forward with our eyes fixed on heaven. And Mary is always there, near those communities, our brothers and sisters; she accompanies them, suffers with them, and sings the *Magnificat* of hope with them.

Mary did not live "with haste," with breathlessness, but, as St. Luke emphasizes, she "kept all these things, pondering them in her heart" (Luke 2:19, 51). Moreover, at the crucial moment of the angel's annunciation, she also asks, "How shall this be?" (Luke 1:34). Yet she does not stop at the moment of reflection, either. She goes a step further: she decides. She does not live in haste but "goes with haste" only when necessary. Mary does not let herself be dragged along by events; she does not avoid the effort of taking a decision. And this happens both in the fundamental decision that was to change her life—"I am the handmaid of the Lord" (Luke 1:38)—and in her daily decisions, routine but also full of meaning. The episode of the wedding at Cana springs to my mind (John 2:1–11): here, too, one sees the realism, humanity, and practicality of Mary, who is attentive to events, to problems.

All this began because "they had no wine." It could all be done because a woman—the Virgin Mary—was attentive, left her concerns in God's hands, and acted sensibly and courageously. But there is a further detail: the best was to come. Everyone went on to enjoy the finest of wines. And this is the good news: the finest wines are yet to be tasted—for families, the richest, deepest, and most beautiful things are yet to come. The time is coming when we will taste love daily, when our children will come to appreciate the home we share, and our elderly will be present each day in the joys of life. The finest of wines is expressed by hope, and this wine will come for every person who stakes everything on love.

And the best wine is yet to come, in spite of all the variables and statistics that say otherwise. The best wine will come to those who today feel hopelessly lost. Say it to yourselves until you are convinced of it. Say it to yourselves, in your hearts: the best wine is yet to come. Whisper it to the hopeless and the loveless. Have patience and hope, and follow Mary's example: pray, open your heart, because the best wine is yet to come. God always seeks out the peripheries, those who have run out of wine, those who drink only of discouragement. Jesus feels their weakness in order to pour out the best wines for those who, for whatever reason, feel that all their jars have been broken.

This is also true in our life: listening to God who speaks to us, and listening also to daily reality, paying attention to people, to events, because the Lord is at the door of our life and knocks in many ways. He puts signs on our path; he gives us the ability to see them. Mary is the Mother of listening, of attentive listening to God and of equally attentive listening to the events of life.

It is difficult to make decisions. We tend to put them off, to let others decide instead. We frequently prefer to let ourselves be dragged along by events, to follow the current fashion. At times we know what we ought to do, but we do not have the courage to do it, or it seems to us too difficult because it means swimming against the tide. In the Annunciation, in the Visitation, and at the wedding at Cana, Mary goes against the tide. Mary goes against the tide; she listens to God, she reflects and seeks to understand reality and decides to entrust herself totally to God. Although she is with child, she decides to visit her elderly relative, and she decides to entrust herself to her Son with insistence so as to preserve the joy of the wedding feast.

This hope, dear brothers and sisters, the hope held out by the Gospel, is the antidote to the spirit of despair that seems to grow like a cancer in societies that are outwardly affluent yet often experience inner sadness and emptiness. Upon how many of our young has this despair taken its toll! May they, the young who surround us in these days with their joy and confidence, never be robbed of their hope!

[The book of Revelation] presents a dramatic scene: a woman—an image of Mary and the Church—is being pursued by a Dragon—the devil—who wants to devour her child. But the scene is not one of death but of life, because God intervenes and saves the child (cf. Rev. 12:13, 15–16). How many difficulties are present in the life of every individual, among our people, in our communities. Yet as great as these may seem, God never allows us to be overwhelmed by them. In the face of those moments of discouragement we experience . . . in our efforts to evangelize or to embody our faith as parents within the family, I would like to say forcefully: Always know in your heart that God is by your side; he never abandons you! Let us never lose hope! Let us never allow it to die in our hearts!

Dear brothers and sisters, let us be lights of hope! Let us maintain a positive outlook on reality. Let us encourage the generosity that is typical of the young and help them work actively in building a better world. Young people are a powerful engine for the Church and for society. They do not need material things alone; also and above all, they need to have held up to them those nonmaterial values that are the spiritual heart of a people, the memory of a people. In the Shrine [of Our Lady of the Conception of Aparecida], which is part of the memory of Brazil, we can almost read those values: spirituality, generosity, solidarity, perseverance, fraternity, joy; they are values whose deepest root is in the Christian faith.

Anyone who is a man or a woman of hope—the great hope that faith gives us—knows that even in the midst of difficulties God acts and he surprises us. The history of *Our Lady of the Conception of Aparecida* is a good example. Three fishermen, after a day of catching no fish, found something unexpected in the waters of the Parnaíba River: an image of Our Lady of the Immaculate Conception. Whoever would have thought that the site of a fruitless fishing expedition would become the place where all Brazilians can feel that they are children of one Mother? God always surprises us, like the new wine in the Gospel we have just heard. God always saves the best for us. But he asks us to let ourselves be surprised by his love, to accept his surprises. Let us trust God! Cut off from him, the wine of joy, the wine of hope, runs out. If we draw near to him, if we stay with him, what seems to be cold water, difficulty, sin, is changed into the new wine of friendship with him.

Dear friends, if we walk in hope, allowing ourselves to be surprised by the new wine Jesus offers us, we have joy in our hearts, and we cannot fail to be witnesses of this joy. Christians are joyful; they are never gloomy. God is at our side. We have a Mother who always intercedes for the life of her children. Jesus has shown us that the face of God is that of a loving Father. Sin and death have been defeated. Christians cannot be pessimists! They do not look like someone in constant mourning. If we are truly in love with Christ and if we sense how much he loves us, our heart will "light up" with a joy that spreads to everyone around us.

Do we think that Jesus' incarnation is simply a past event that has nothing to do with us personally? Believing in Jesus means giving him our flesh with the humility and courage of Mary, so that he can continue to dwell in our midst. It means giving him our hands, to caress the little ones and the poor; our feet, to go forth and meet our brothers and sisters; our arms, to hold up the weak and to work in the Lord's vineyard; our minds, to think and act in the light of the Gospel; and especially to offer our hearts to love and to make choices in accordance with God's will. All this happens thanks to the working of the Holy Spirit. And in this way we become instruments in God's hands, so that Jesus can act in the world through us.

At the end of its Constitution on the Church, the Second Vatican Council left us a very beautiful meditation on Mary Most Holy. Let me just recall the words referring to the mystery we celebrate today: "The immaculate Virgin preserved free from all stain of original sin, was taken up body and soul into heavenly glory, when her earthly life was over, and exalted by the Lord as Queen over all things" (no. 59). Then toward the end, there is, "The Mother of Jesus in the glory which she possesses in body and soul in heaven is the image and the beginning of the Church as it is to be perfected in the world to come. Likewise, she shines forth on earth, until the day of the Lord shall come."

Endnotes

Page 1: The apostles, who saw the risen Christ . . . Regina Caeli, April 19, 2015. (www.vatican.va).

Page 1: We may ask ourselves: Who is a witness? . . . Regina Caeli, April 19, 2015. (www.vatican.va).

Page 1: Today all of us are in continuity with that group of apostles . . . General Audience, September 17, 2014. (www.vatican.va).

Page 2: Jesus begins his mission not only from . . . Angelus, January 26, 2014. (www.vatican.va).

Page 2: The content of Christian witness is not a theory. . . . Regina Caeli, April 19, 2015. (www.vatican.va).

Page 2: But Jesus is present also through the Church, . . . Regina Caeli, June 1, 2014. (www.vatican.va).

Page 3: The Gospel is the word of life. . . . Angelus, February 1, 2015. (www.vatican.va).

Page 3: [Galilee] is a borderland, a place of transit . . . Angelus, January 26, 2014. (www.vatican.va).

Page 3: Starting from Galilee, Jesus teaches us . . . Angelus, January 26, 2014. (www.vatican.va).

Page 3: Jesus calls his disciples and sends them out . . . Homily, July 12, 2015. (www.vatican.va).

Page 4: Let us think about some of these attitudes . . . Homily, July 12, 2015. (www.vatican.va).

Page 4: Jesus does not send them out as men of influence . . . Homily, July 12, 2015. (www.vatican.va).

Page 4: Jesus sends his disciples out to all nations . . . Homily for Canonization Mass for Junípero Serra, September 23, 2015. (www.vatican.va).

Page 5: Jesus said, Go out and tell the good news . . . Homily for Canonization Mass for Junípero Serra, September 23, 2015. (www.vatican.va).

Page 5: All the goods that we have received are to [be given] . . . Angelus, November 16, 2014. (www.vatican.va).

Page 5: [We are] not to conceal our faith and our belonging to Christ . . . Angelus, November 16, 2014. (www.vatican.va).

Page 6: To his missionary disciples Jesus says, . . . Regina Caeli, June 1, 2014. (www.vatican.va).

Page 6: In the voice of Jesus who tells him, "Come!" . . . Angelus, August 10, 2014. (www.vatican.va).

Page 6: And the final scene is also very important. . . . Angelus, August 10, 2014. (www.vatican.va).

Page 6: Dear friends, the Lord is calling today too! . . . Angelus, January 26, 2014. (www.vatican.va).

Page 7: The Church, the holy People of God, . . . Homily for Canonization Mass for Junípero Serra, September 23, 2015. (www.vatican.va).

Page 7: [On] this journey, ever guided by the Word of God . . . Regina Caeli, April 19, 2015. (www.vatican.va).

Page 7: Listen to Jesus. He is the Savior . . . Angelus, March 1, 2015. (www.vatican.va).

Page 9: At the baptism, the Holy Spirit descended . . . Homily, May 24, 2014. (www.vatican.va).

Page 9: Then the Holy Spirit descends in the form of a dove . . . Angelus, January 11, 2015. (www.vatican.va).

Page 9: To subject our Christian life and mission . . . Angelus, January 11, 2015. (www.vatican.va).

Page 10: The Pentecost of the Upper Room in Jerusalem . . . Homily, May 19, 2013. (www.vatican.va).

Page 10: "As the Father has sent me, even so I send you . . . Homily, May 24, 2015. (www.vatican.va).

Page 10: As a result, "all of them were filled with the Holy Spirit," . . . Homily, May 19, 2013. (www.vatican.va).

Page 11: This event, which changes the heart and life . . . Regina Caeli, May 24, 2015. (www.vatican.va).

Page 11: The Church is not born isolated . . . Regina Caeli, May 24, 2015. (www.vatican.va).

Page 11: A fundamental element of Pentecost is *astonishment* . . . Regina Caeli, June 8, 2014. (www.vatican.va).

Page 11: The Church born at Pentecost is an astounding community . . . Regina Caeli, June 8, 2014. (www.vatican.va).

Page 12: The Holy Spirit would appear to create disorder . . . Homily, May 19, 2013. (www.vatican.va).

Page 12: If we let ourselves be guided by the Spirit . . . Homily, May 19, 2013. (www.vatican.va).

Page 12: The Holy Spirit also *anoints* . . . Homily, May 24, 2014. (www.vatican.va).

Page 13: This was the experience of the apostle Paul . . . Homily, June 16, 2013. (www.vatican.va).

Page 13: The Christian is someone who thinks and acts . . . Homily, June 16, 2013. (www.vatican.va).

Page 13: The world needs men and women who are not closed . . . Homily, May 24, 2015. (www.vatican.va).

Page 14: In the Christian perspective, a charism . . . General Audience, October 1, 2014. (www.vatican.va).

Page 14: An important thing that should be highlighted . . . General Audience, October 1, 2014. (www.vatican.va).

Page 14: So, each one of us should ask himself or herself . . . General Audience, October 1, 2014. (www.vatican.va).

Page 14: The most beautiful experience . . . General Audience, October 1, 2014. (www.vatican.va).

Page 15: When the Holy Spirit comes to dwell in our hearts . . . General Audience, June 11, 2014. (www.vatican.va).

Page 15: The Church is called into being forever . . . Regina Caeli, June 8, 2014. (www.vatican.va).

Page 15: As on that day of Pentecost, the Holy Spirit . . . Regina Caeli, St. Peter's Square, May 24, 2015. (www.vatican.va).

Page 17: What is the image we have of God? . . . Homily, June 16, 2013. (www.vatican.va).

Page 17: "And God saw that it was good" . . . Homily, September 7, 2013. (www.vatican.va).

Page 17: We can ask ourselves: what does this message mean? . . . Homily, September 7, 2013. (www.vatican.va).

Page 18: God's world is a world in which everyone . . . Homily, September 7, 2013. (www.vatican.va).

Page 18: But then we wonder, Is this the world . . . Homily, September 7, 2013. (www.vatican.va).

Page 18: When man thinks only of himself . . . Homily, September 7, 2013. (www.vatican.va).

Page 18: "Adam, where are you?" . . . Homily, July 8, 2013. (www.vatican.va).

Page 19: It is exactly in this chaos that God asks . . . Homily, September 7, 2013. (www.vatican.va).

Page 19: This is not a question of coincidence but the truth . . . Homily, September 7, 2013. (www.vatican.va).

Page 19: God chooses Abraham, our father in faith . . . General Audience, June 18, 2014. (www.vatican.va).

Page 20: Abraham and his own listen to the call of God . . . General Audience, June 18, 2014. (www.vatican.va).

Page 20: *Walking*. This verb makes us reflect on . . . Homily, December 24, 2013. (www.vatican.va).

Page 20: [In] the calling of Moses . . . Homily, June 16, 2013. (www.vatican.va).

Page 21: [This is] the ancient prayer of blessing . . . Homily, January 1, 2014. (www.vatican.va).

Page 21: "The Lord your God . . . fed you with manna . . . Homily, June 19, 2014. (www.vatican.va).

Page 22: The prophet Hosea says, "I have walked with you . . . General Audience, June 18, 2014. (www.vatican.va).

Page 22: Dear friends, this is God's plan . . . General Audience, June 18, 2014. (www.vatican.va).

Page 22: "The people who walked in darkness . . . Homily, December 24, 2013. (www.vatican.va).

Page 23: The prophet Isaiah is addressing a people . . . Homily, July 7, 2013. (www.vatican.va).

Page 23: Every Christian, and especially you or I . . . Homily, July 7, 2013. (www.vatican.va).

Page 25: Jesus pronounces a prophecy . . . Angelus, March 22, 2015. (www.vatican.va).

Page 25: The same Peter who professed Jesus Christ . . . Homily, March 14, 2013. (www.vatican.va).

Page 25: According to an ancient Roman tradition . . . Address, July 26, 2013. (www.vatican.va).

Page 26: To those who, today too, "wish to see Jesus . . . Angelus, March 22, 2015. (www.vatican.va).

Page 26: Today's Gospel presents the episode . . . Angelus, March 8, 2015. (www.vatican.va).

Page 26: They were seeking a divine and prodigious sign . . . Angelus, March 8, 2015. (www.vatican.va).

Page 27: God placed on Jesus' Cross all the weight . . . Good Friday Address, April 18, 2014. (www.vatican.va).

Page 27: Jesus is united with every person . . . Address, July 26, 2013. (www.vatican.va).

Page 27: How our inconsistencies make Jesus suffer! . . . Address, July 26, 2013. (www.vatican.va).

Page 28: Do you want to be like Pilate, . . . Address, July 26, 2013. (www.vatican.va).

Page 28: Today's Gospel again offers us the words that Jesus . . . Angelus, March 15, 2015. (www.vatican.va).

Page 28: According to the evangelist John . . . Angelus, March 8, 2015. (www.vatican.va).

Page 28: While we contemplate and celebrate the Holy Cross . . . Angelus, September 14, 2014. (www.vatican.va).

Page 29: Let us walk in the world as Jesus did . . . Angelus, March 8, 2015. (www.vatican.va).

Page 29: But Jesus never strikes [us]. . . . Angelus, March 8, 2015. (www.vatican.va).

Page 29: Why was the Cross necessary? . . . Angelus, September 14, 2014. (www.vatican.va).

Page 29: When we look to the Cross . . . Angelus, September 14, 2014. (www.vatican.va).

Page 30: Before the Cross of Jesus, we apprehend . . . Good Friday address, April 18, 2014. (www.vatican.va).

Page 30: On Calvary, there at the foot of the Cross . . . Angelus, September 14, 2014. (www.vatican.va).

Page 30: St. Paul reminds us, "God, who is rich . . . Angelus, March 15, 2015. (www.vatican.va).

Page 31: The Cross is the word through which . . . Good Friday address, March 29, 2013. (www.vatican.va).

Page 31: Impress, Lord, in our hearts the sentiments . . . Good Friday address, April 3, 2015. (www.vatican.va).

Page 31: Jesus Crucified, strengthen faith in us . . . Good Friday address, April 3, 2015. (www.vatican.va).

Page 31: The Cross of Christ contains all the love of God . . . Address, July 26, 2013. (www.vatican.va).

Page 33: [May we worship] him! . . . Basilica of Saint Paul Outside-the-Walls, April 14, 2013. (www.vatican.va).

Page 33: What does it mean, then, to worship God? . . . Basilica of Saint Paul Outside-the-Walls, April 14, 2013. (www.vatican.va).

Page 33: The woman [at the well] asks Jesus . . . Homily, January 25, 2015. (www.vatican.va).

Page 34: We have to empty ourselves of the many small . . . Basilica of Saint Paul Outside-the-Walls, April 14, 2013. (www.vatican.va).

Page 34: [On the feast of Corpus Christi] the Church praises the Lord . . . Homily, June 21, 2014. (www.vatican.va).

Page 34: First of all we are *a people who adore God* . . . Homily, June 21, 2014. (www.vatican.va).

Page 34: Let us confess . . . as we turn our gaze . . . Homily, June 21, 2014. (www.vatican.va).

Page 35: Our faith in the true presence of Jesus Christ . . . Homily, June 21, 2014. (www.vatican.va).

Page 35: The Lord Jesus never ceases to inspire acts . . . Homily, June 21, 2014. (www.vatican.va).

Page 35: Dear brothers and sisters, the Eucharist . . . Homily, June 21, 2014. (www.vatican.va).

Page 35: Christian unity—we are convinced . . . Homily, January 25, 2015. (www.vatican.va).

Page 35: On the occasion of Jewish Passover . . . Homily, March 7, 2015. (www.vatican.va).

Page 36: This act of Jesus *is an act of cleansing* . . . Homily, March 7, 2015. (www.vatican.va).

Page 36: The liturgy [is] "the primary and indispensable . . . Homily, March 7, 2015. (www.vatican.va).

Page 36: Therefore, the Church calls us . . . Homily, March 7, 2015. (www.vatican.va).

Page 37: [Our liturgy] is about fulfilling an itinerary . . . Homily, March 7, 2015. (www.vatican.va).

Page 37: A disciple of Jesus does not go . . . Homily, March 7, 2015. (www.vatican.va).

Page 37: The prayer of praise is a Christian prayer . . . Address, October 31, 2014. (www.vatican.va).

Page 38: Together with the prayer of praise . . . Address, October 31, 2014. (www.vatican.va).

Page 38: This relationship with the Lord is . . . General Audience, June 4, 2014. (www.vatican.va).

Page 38: In the Letter to the Romans the apostle Paul states . . . General Audience, June 4, 2014. (www.vatican.va).

Page 38: Prayer expresses what we experience . . . Address, July 11, 2015. (www.vatican.va).

Page 39: Prayer is the reflection of our love for God . . . Address, July 11, 2015. (www.vatican.va).

Page 39: If the gift of piety makes us grow . . . General Audience, June 4, 2014. (www.vatican.va).

Page 39: The gift of piety means to be truly capable . . . General Audience, June 4, 2014. (www.vatican.va).

Page 41: It is not Abraham who builds about himself a people . . . General Audience, June 18, 2014. (www.vatican.va).

Page 41: God forms a people with all those who listen . . . General Audience, June 18, 2014. (www.vatican.va).

Page 41: When we arrive, God is waiting for us . . . General Audience, June 18, 2014. (www.vatican.va).

Page 42: We become accustomed to living . . . General Audience, March 5, 2014. (www.vatican.va).

Page 42: The family prays . . . Homily, October 27, 2013. (www.vatican.va).

Page 42: The prayer of the tax collector . . . Homily, October 27, 2013. (www.vatican.va).

Page 42: But in the family how is this done? . . . Homily, October 27, 2013. (www.vatican.va).

Page 43: Then, at home, your son wants to talk . . . General Audience, November 19, 2014. (www.vatican.va).

Page 43: Dear grandparents, dear elderly . . . General Audience, March 11, 2015. (www.vatican.va).

Page 44: Prayer *unceasingly purifies the heart* . . . General Audience, March 11, 2015. (www.vatican.va).

Page 44: John's Gospel states that, before his Passion . . . General Audience, October 30, 2013. (www.vatican.va).

Page 44: The Gospel presents Jesus in dialogue . . . General Audience, October 30, 2013. 20, 2015. (www.vatican.va).

Page 45: It is so beautiful to know that the Lord . . . General Audience, August 27, 2014. (www.vatican.va).

Page 45: The first reassurance we have . . . General Audience, August 27, 2014. (www.vatican.va).

Page 45: Jesus prays and he invites us to pray . . . General Audience, October 30, 2013. (www.vatican.va).

Page 45: When we receive and welcome him . . . General Audience, May 7, 2014. (www.vatican.va).

Page 46: The Spirit helps us to grow . . . General Audience, May 7, 2014. (www.vatican.va).

Page 46: There must never be a shortage of prayer . . . General Audience, October 8, 2014. (www.vatican.va).

Page 46: In the Gospel we hear, "Pray therefore . . . Homily, July 7, 2013. (www.vatican.va).

Page 46: The Church, as Pope Benedict XVI . . . Homily, July 7, 2013. (www.vatican.va).

Page 47: The passage from Revelation 12:1–6 . . . Homily, August 15, 2013. (www.vatican.va).

Page 47: Mary walks with us always . . . Homily, August 15, 2013. (www.vatican.va).

Page 49: One of the great gifts from the Second Vatican Council . . . General Audience, November 19, 2014. (www.vatican.va).

Page 49: The Church, the "advocate of justice . . . Address, July 25, 2013. (www.vatican.va).

Page 49: There is neither real promotion of the common good . . . Address, July 25, 2013. (www.vatican.va).

Page 50: Our recent past has been marked by the concern . . . Address, November 25, 2014. (www.vatican.va).

Page 50: The common home of all men and women . . . Address, September 25, 2015. (www.vatican.va).

Page 50: To enable real men and women to escape . . . Address, September 25, 2015. (www.vatican.va).

Page 50: Today, the number of young people . . . Address, February 28, 2014. (www.vatican.va).

Page 51: In the throwaway culture, we find . . . Address, February 28, 2014. (www.vatican.va).

Page 51: I think that this moment is the most pronounced . . . Address, July 12, 2014. (www.vatican.va).

Page 51: The aim, therefore, is to save man . . . Address, July 12, 2014. (www.vatican.va).

Page 52: [Along with the] lives thrown away . . . Address, January 12, 2015. (www.vatican.va).

Page 52: Our world is facing a refugee crisis . . . Speech, September 24, 2015. (www.vatican.va).

Page 52: As long as everyone seeks to accumulate . . . Angelus, March 2, 2014. (www.vatican.va).

Page 53: A heart troubled by the desire for possessions . . . Angelus, March 2, 2014. (www.vatican.va).

Page 53: If each of us accumulates not for ourselves . . . Angelus, March 2, 2014. (www.vatican.va).

Page 53: Peace is threatened by every denial . . . Address, January 13, 2014. (www.vatican.va).

Page 53: In the end, what kind of dignity . . . Address, November 25, 2014. (www.vatican.va).

Page 54: Promoting the dignity of the person . . . Address, November 25, 2014. (www.vatican.va).

Page 54: Today there is a tendency to claim . . . Address, November 25, 2014. (www.vatican.va).

Page 54: It is vital to develop a culture . . . Address, November 25, 2014. (www.vatican.va).

Page 54: To speak of *transcendent human dignity* . . . Address, November 25, 2014. (www.vatican.va).

Page 55: We encounter certain rather selfish lifestyles . . . Address, November 25, 2014. (www.vatican.va).

Page 55: This is the great mistake made . . . Address, November 25, 2014. (www.vatican.va).

Page 55: To give . . . hope means more than simply . . . Address, November 25, 2014. (www.vatican.va).

Page 56: The time has come to promote policies . . . Address, November 25, 2014. (www.vatican.va).

Page 57: God's heart has a special place for the poor . . . *Evangelii Gaudium*, 197. (www.vatican.va).

Page 57: When he began to preach the Kingdom . . . *Evangelii Gaudium*, 197. (www.vatican.va).

Page 57: The proclamation of the Gospel is destined . . . Address, June 17, 2013. (www.vatican.va).

Page 58: The poor are at the center of the Gospel . . . Homily, January 16, 2015. (www.vatican.va).

Page 58: If the whole Church takes up this missionary impulse . . . *Evangelii Gaudium*, 48. (www.vatican.va).

Page 58: The poor are also the privileged teachers . . . Address, September 10, 2013. (www.vatican.va).

Page 59: The Church, which is missionary by her nature . . . Address, May 9, 2014. (www.vatican.va).

Page 59: The poor person, when loved . . . *Evangelii Gaudium*, 199. (www.vatican.va).

Page 59: There are many poor families who . . . General Audience, June 3, 2015. (www.vatican.va).

Page 60: We Christians have to be ever closer . . . General Audience, June 3, 2015. (www.vatican.va).

Page 60: Each individual Christian and every community . . . *Evangelii Gaudium*, 187. (www.vatican.va).

Page 60: If we, who are God's means . . . *Evangelii Gaudium*, 187. (www.vatican.va).

Page 61: Jesus [invites us]: "Come to me . . . Angelus, July 6, 2014. (www.vatican.va).

Page 61: The Church is mother and must not . . . General Audience, June 3, 2015. (www.vatican.va).

Page 61: The Gospel of Matthew presents to us . . . Angelus, August 3, 2014. (www.vatican.va).

Page 62: We can understand three messages . . . Angelus, August 3, 2014. (www.vatican.va).

Page 62: Jesus is like this: he suffers . . . Angelus, August 3, 2014. (www.vatican.va).

Page 62: The first [message of this event] is compassion . . . Angelus, August 3, 2014. (www.vatican.va).

Page 63: How many times we turn away . . . Angelus, August 3, 2014. (www.vatican.va).

Page 63: The miracle of the loaves foreshadows . . . Angelus, August 3, 2014. (www.vatican.va).

Page 63: The goodness of God has no bounds . . . Angelus, October 12, 2014. (www.vatican.va).

Page 63: The Last Supper represents the culmination . . . Angelus, June 7, 2015. (www.vatican.va).

Page 64: The Christ, who nourishes us . . . Angelus, June 7, 2015. (www.vatican.va).

Page 65: It must be stated that a true "right of the environment" . . . Address, September 25, 2015. (www.vatican.va).

Page 65: Any harm done to the environment . . . Address, September 25, 2015. (www.vatican.va).

Page 65: [In Revelation 7:3] we heard this voice . . . Homily, November 1, 2014. (www.vatican.va).

Page 66: Man takes control of everything . . . Homily, November 1, 2014. (www.vatican.va).

Page 66: Never more than at this moment . . . Message for World Food Day, 2014. (www.vatican.va).

Page 66: Sharing means to be a neighbor . . . Message for World Food Day, 2014. (www.vatican.va).

Page 67: To defeat hunger, it is not enough . . . Message for World Food Day, 2014. (www.vatican.va).

Page 67: How long will we continue to defend systems . . . Message for World Food Day, 2014. (www.vatican.va).

Page 67: It goes without saying that part of this great . . . Address, September 24, 2015. (www.vatican.va).

Page 67: Now is the time for courageous actions . . . Address, September 24, 2015. (www.vatican.va).

Page 68: [The] culture of care for the environment . . . Statement, Synod Hall, July 21, 2015. (www.vatican.va).

Page 68: [I]n society, in the social life of mankind . . . Statement, Synod Hall, July 21, 2015. (www.vatican.va).

Page 68: One of the most notable things . . . Statement, Synod Hall, July 21, 2015. (www.vatican.va).

Page 68: [The idolatry of] technocracy leads to . . . Statement, Synod Hall, July 21, 2015. (www.vatican.va).

Page 69: What happens when all these phenomena . . . Statement, Synod Hall, July 21, 2015. (www.vatican.va).

Page 69: I refer in particular to the agricultural environment . . . Statement, Synod Hall, July 21, 2015. (www.vatican.va).

Page 69: [Romano Guardini] speaks of two forms of ignorance . . . Statement, Synod Hall, July 21, 2015. (www.vatican.va).

Page 69: Atomic energy is good; it can be helpful . . . Statement, Synod Hall, July 21, 2015. (www.vatican.va).

Page 70: The vocation of being a "protector," . . . Homily, March 19, 2013. (www.vatican.va).

Page 70: Please, I would like to ask all . . . Homily, March 19, 2013. (www.vatican.va).

Page 71: Our earth needs constant concern and attention . . . Address, November 25, 2014. (www.vatican.va).

Page 71: Respect for the environment, . . . Address, November 25, 2014. (www.vatican.va).

Page 71: Our attitude . . . is the attitude of the Beatitudes. . . . Homily, November 1, 2014. (www.vatican.va).

Page 73: The family is in crisis: . . . Address, March 21, 2015. (www.vatican.va).

Page 73: Preparing for marriage is not like taking a class . . . Address, March 21, 2015. (www.vatican.va).

Page 74: Let us think about our parents, . . . Address, October 4, 2013. (www.vatican.va).

Page 74: Yes, it is so true that it takes courage . . . Address, October 4, 2013. (www.vatican.va).

Page 74: With trust in God's faithfulness, . . . Address, October 26, 2013. (www.vatican.va).

Page 75: "*In joy and in sadness, in sickness and in health. . . .*" Address, October 26, 2013. (www.vatican.va).

Page 75: In order to have a healthy family, three phrases . . . Address, October 26, 2013. (www.vatican.va).

Page 75: In marriage there is also fighting . . . Address, March 21, 2015. (www.vatican.va).

Page 76: It is always important to ask the other . . . Address, March 21, 2015. (www.vatican.va).

Page 76: Dear parents, your children need to discover . . . Address, June 14, 2015. (www.vatican.va).

Page 76: There is no greater testimony for a child . . . Address, June 14, 2015. (www.vatican.va).

Page 76: You are collaborators with the Holy Spirit . . . Address, June 14, 2015. (www.vatican.va).

Page 77: Let us think how much children suffer . . . Address, June 14, 2015. (www.vatican.va).

Page 77: [Some children are] orphans, without the memory . . . Address, June 16, 2014. (www.vatican.va).

Page 78: Are grandparents given a place of dignity . . . Address, June 14, 2015. (www.vatican.va).

Page 78: I'm sure I've already told this story, . . . Address, June 14, 2015. (www.vatican.va).

Page 78: We live nowadays in immense cities . . . Address, October 28, 2014. (www.vatican.va).

Page 79: I said it, and I repeat it: a home for every family. . . . Address, October 28, 2014. (www.vatican.va).

Page 79: Let yourselves be healed by Jesus. . . . Homily, February 8, 2015. (www.vatican.va).

Page 79: For this reason I say to each one of you: . . . Homily, February 8, 2015. (www.vatican.va).

Page 81: I would like to talk about the child . . . General Audience, February 11, 2015. (www.vatican.va).

Page 81: We must consider this carefully . . . General Audience, February 11, 2015. (www.vatican.va).

Page 81: First of all children remind us . . . General Audience, March 18, 2015. (www.vatican.va).

Page 82: It is not by chance that in the Gospel . . . General Audience, March 18, 2015. (www.vatican.va).

Page 82: Once Jesus rebuked his disciples . . . General Audience, April 8, 2015. (www.vatican.va).

Page 82: [Mark chapter five] presents the account . . . Angelus, June 28, 2015. (www.vatican.va).

Page 83: Children are in and of themselves a treasure . . . General Audience, March 18, 2015. (www.vatican.va).

Page 83: We are all sons and daughters . . . General Audience, March 18, 2015. (www.vatican.va).

Page 83: A child has spontaneous trust in his father and mother . . . General Audience, March 18, 2015. (www.vatican.va).

Page 84: Children have the capacity to smile . . . General Audience, March 18, 2015. (www.vatican.va).

Page 84: Despite our seemingly evolved sensitivity . . . General Audience, June 24, 2015. (www.vatican.va).

Page 84: The weakness and suffering of our dearest . . . General Audience, June 10, 2015. (www.vatican.va).

Page 85: From the first moments of their lives . . . General Audience, April 8, 2015. (www.vatican.va).

Page 85: Every child who is marginalized, abandoned . . . General Audience, April 8, 2015. (www.vatican.va).

Page 86: A mother then thinks of the health of her children . . . Address, May 4, 2013. (www.vatican.va).

Page 86: A child is loved because he is one's child . . . General Audience, February 11, 2015. (www.vatican.va).

Page 86: Think what a society would be like . . . General Audience, April 8, 2015. (www.vatican.va).

Page 86: [There is] depth in the human experience . . . General Audience, February 11, 2015. (www.vatican.va).

Page 87: In a frail human being, each one of us . . . Address, September 20, 2013. (www.vatican.va).

Page 87: The fourth commandment asks children . . . General Audience, February 11, 2015. (www.vatican.va).

Page 87: May the Lord bless our parents . . . General Audience, February 11, 2015. (www.vatican.va).

Page 89: How was Mary's faith a journey? . . . Address, October 12, 2013. (www.vatican.va).

Page 89: Mary was always with Jesus . . . Address, October 12, 2013. (www.vatican.va).

Page 89: Our pilgrimage of faith has been inseparably . . . Homily, January 1, 2014. (www.vatican.va).

Page 90: The "woman" became our Mother . . . Homily, January 1, 2014. (www.vatican.va).

Page 90: In celebrating [the Assumption], . . . Homily, August 15, 2014. (www.vatican.va).

Page 90: We can imagine that the Virgin Mary . . . Homily, September 28, 2014. (www.vatican.va).

Page 91: Mary is not in a hurry, . . . Address, May 31, 2013. (www.vatican.va).

Page 91: What gave rise to Mary's act of going . . . Address, May 31, 2013. (www.vatican.va).

Page 91: We heard the Song of Mary . . . Homily, Castel Gandolfo, August 15, 2013. (www.vatican.va).

Page 92: For us Christians, wherever the Cross is . . . Homily, Castel Gandolfo, August 15, 2013. (www.vatican.va).

Page 92: Mary did not live "with haste," . . . Address, May 31, 2013. (www.vatican.va).

Page 92: All this began because "they had no wine . . . Homily, July 6, 2015. (www.vatican.va).

Page 92: And the best wine is yet to come . . . Homily, July 6, 2015. (www.vatican.va).

Page 93: This is also true in our life . . . Address, May 31, 2013. (www.vatican.va).

Page 93: It is difficult to make decisions . . . Address, May 31, 2013. (www.vatican.va).

Page 93: This hope, dear brothers and sisters . . . Homily, August 15, 2014. (www.vatican.va).

Page 93: [The book of Revelation] presents a dramatic scene . . . Homily, July 24, 2013. (www.vatican.va).

Page 94: Dear brothers and sisters, let us be lights of hope . . . Homily, July 24, 2013. (www.vatican.va).

Page 94: Anyone who is a man or a woman of hope . . . Homily, July 24, 2013. (www.vatican.va).

Page 94: Dear friends, if we walk in hope . . . Homily, July 24, 2013. (www.vatican.va).

Page 95: Do we think that Jesus' incarnation . . . Address, October 12, 2013. (www.vatican.va).

Page 95: At the end of its Constitution on the Church . . . Homily, Castel Gandolfo, August 15, 2013. (www.vatican.va).

About the Editor and Compiler

James P. Campbell has over 40 years of experience as a catechist and national speaker in Catholic religious education. He received a BA and an MA degree in European History and later an MA in theology and a Doctor of Ministry in Christian Education from Aquinas Institute of Theology.

In the 12 years prior to retirement, Jim was Staff Theologian at Loyola Press. He is the coauthor of *Finding God: Our Response to God's Gifts*, Grades 1–8. Jim has also written *The Stories of the Old Testament: A Catholic's Guide* and *Mary and the Saints: Companions on the Journey*.

Other Books by Pope Francis

The Church of Mercy
A Vision for the Church

Collected from Pope Francis's speeches, homilies, and papers presented during the first year of his papacy, *The Church of Mercy* is the first Vatican-authorized book detailing his vision for the Catholic Church.

Paperback | 4170-3 | $16.95
Hardcover | 4168-0 | $22.95

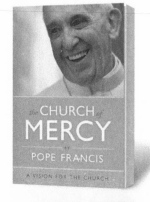

Walking with Jesus
A Way Forward for the Church

In *Walking with Jesus: A Way Forward for the Church*, Pope Francis urges us to make Jesus central in our individual lives and in the collective life of the Church.

Paperback | 4254-0 | $16.95
Hardcover | 4248-9 | $22.95

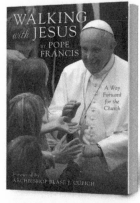

The Joy of Discipleship
Reflections from Pope Francis
on Walking with Christ

The Joy of Discipleship includes reflections from Pope Francis on what it means to be a true disciple of Jesus, and how discipleship can frame and form our everyday lives as Christians.

Paperback | 4431-5 | $16.95
Hardcover | 4387-5 | $22.95

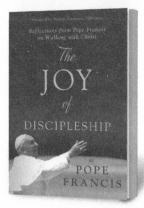

TO ORDER: Call 800.621.1008, visit www.loyolapress.com/store, or visit your local bookseller.

Learn More About Pope Francis's Message of Mercy

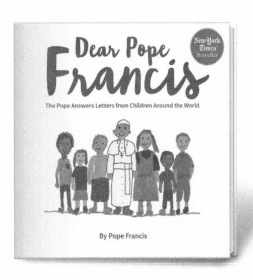
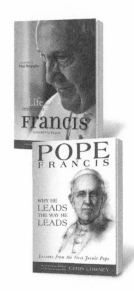